En Route to Modern Growth: Latin America in the 1990s

Essays in Honor of Carlos Díaz-Alejandro

Gustav Ranis
Editor

Published by the Inter-American Development Bank
Distributed by The Johns Hopkins University Press

Washington, D.C.
1994

HC
123
E6
1994

The views and opinions expressed in this publication are those of the
authors and do not reflect the official position of the Inter-American
Development Bank.

En Route to Modern Growth: Latin America in the 1990s

Essays in Honor of Carlos Díaz-Alejandro

© Copyright 1994 by the Inter-American Development Bank

Inter-American Development Bank
1300 New York Ave., NW
Washington, DC 20577

Distributed by
The Johns Hopkins University Press
2715 North Charles Street
Baltimore, MD 21218-4319

Library of Congress Catalog Card Number: 94-78309
ISBN 0-940602-85-7

PREFACE

This book contains a selection of studies presented at a colloquium entitled "En Route to Modern Growth: Latin America in the 1990s," which was held in May 1993 at the Inter-American Development Bank's headquarters in Washington, D.C. Both the conference and this book are dedicated to the memory of Carlos Díaz-Alejandro.

As editor Gustav Ranis explains with great care in his introduction, Carlos was a man whose contributions to the understanding of development and economics have always been highly regarded for their academic and theoretical content. For years his work has served as both an inspiration and a point of departure for all those involved in the study of Latin American economic development.

In order to pay proper tribute to Carlos, we must study his work carefully, learn from it, encourage debate, and continue from where he left off. It is in this spirit that we dedicate this work.

Nohra Rey de Marulanda
Manager
Integration and Regional Programs Department

TABLE OF CONTENTS

INTRODUCTION

Carlos Díaz-Alejandro: Historian and Prophet
Gustav Ranis

Economists like to joke about the fact that we are much better at predicting the past than the future. The reality is that we would be much better off if we could just predict the past a bit more accurately and thus be in a position to learn more from it.

Carlos Díaz-Alejandro, whose memory we are honoring by means of this present volume, didn't have this problem. He was and remains an exception. Carlos was a bridge builder, not only between North and South, as has been frequently commented upon, but also between the past and the future. This is evident in much of his work, including his contributions to the topics under discussion here.

Carlos undoubtedly would have particularly enjoyed participating in this discussion on the relative roles of government and markets in development, partly because this debate has gradually become much more nuanced than what it was earlier: an oversimplified contest between the structuralist import-substitution school, in retreat, against the neo-classical troops, on the offensive, under the banner of the "Washington Consensus." I for one believe that today he would be insisting on the evolution of a hemispheric rather than a Washington consensus, stressing the fact that markets, once we leave pristine textbook versions behind, are far from perfect, and that governments are by no means universally evil and/or inept. I would, moreover, venture to guess that by now he would have presented the profession with a much more subtle statement of what the ideal division of labor between government and markets should look like, given the experience of distant and not-so-distant history. In other words, he would today be trying to put more content into the recently coined "market friendly" interventions motto, put out by the Washington Consensus people who find themselves in some slight, but still orderly, tactical retreat.

Let me cite a few clues as to what I believe Carlos might be saying to us today. He long ago noted that "markets in which international transactions take place historically are rigged against the less-developed countries [LDCs]." Without falling into extreme traps of the type offered by the United Nations Conference on Trade and Development, he was not afraid to question the myth of the seven-foot-tall international market disciplinarian required to keep domestic policy/makers honest. It is my guess that he would have viewed the current penchant for privatization with a similar dose of skepticism, perhaps insisting on some assurance that privatization be accompanied by an increasingly workable and competitive market structure, rather than one which runs the risk of exchanging public for private monopoly.

On the other hand, we must also not forget that Carlos was a member of the National Bureau of Economic Research's project on trade liberalization, which was directed by Anne Krueger, the high priestess of the neoclassical Washington Consensus, or that he wrote extensively on liberalization packages and liberalization sequences in the Southern Cone, in veins not very different from those of Sebastian Edwards, Vittorio Corbo, and others. What distinguishes him from the ordinary economist, however, is not only that he wrote well but that he wrote with subtlety. He was, for example, one of the first to foreshadow some of the current discussion on sustainability and credibility, pointing out that avoiding policy oscillation is likely to be much more important than finding the precise average mix between markets and governments. In this, he clearly anticipates some of the work of Guillermo Calvo and Dani Rodrik.

Carlos was especially concerned about the simultaneous freeing up of the current and capital accounts; indeed, he accurately predicted the negative consequences of such a policy, with the highly mobile factor—capital—causing extreme oscillations, privatized banking systems failing, and governments being forced by foreign pressure to guarantee loans. His advice, that domestic financial liberalization should accompany any move to freer trade but that the removal of exchange controls on foreign capital should come last, could have proven very helpful in many instances. Overall, he saw the merits of a steady course (the "elimination of damaging stop-go cycles") as the highest priority.

It is also of interest to note that Carlos emphasized again and again the asymmetry between the Northern positions on international capital, technology, and labor mobility. The North, he was fond of pointing out, is religious on the first, mixed on the second, but fully heretic when it comes to labor. He was, of course, ready to acknowledge privately that open borders to unskilled labor are not likely to be in the cards anytime soon, if ever, and certainly not when we see even free trade giving way to fair trade as soon as it is clearly no longer in the interest of the main hegemonic power. Nevertheless, the fact is that the seemingly orthogonal trends towards economic globalization, on the one hand, and political separatism, on the other, have caused labor migration to be put on the front burner once again, partly in the context of growing legal and illegal migration into Western Europe, the United States, and Japan, and partly with respect to the newly industrialized countries of East Asia, which have moved into labor shortage situations during the past decade. I believe Carlos frequently returned to this point about asymmetry not only to twit the Northern establishment, something which he enjoyed doing, of course, but also to achieve a more reasoned response when it came to extolling the virtues of the untrammeled movement of capital.

After all, one of his path-breaking contributions (with Rick Brecher) was to point out that, in the presence of protection, capital inflows such as direct foreign investment (DFI) can, in fact, magnify distortions, enhance the role of trade restrictions, and increase the power of vested interest groups. Such emphasis on the quality rather than the quantity of various types of foreign capital inflows is currently getting increased attention. Contemporary discussions regarding DFI and official development assistance (ODA) are increasingly sensitive to the fact that capital flows from rich to poor may possibly reduce welfare, rather than necessarily enhance it. This is due partly to the domestic distortions Carlos specifically noted, partly to the unfavorable impact they may have on exchange rates (the narrow definition of the "Dutch Disease"), and partly to the adverse political-economy impact they may have on the quality of overall macroeconomic policy (a broader definition of the same illness).

All in all, it is clear that while Carlos was in general agreement with the orthodox trend towards enhanced market orientation in countries that are heavily distorted during import-substitution regimes, he clearly wanted to move beyond the basic Washington Consensus. Today he would undoubtedly be specifying precisely what sorts of government institution-building and regulatory frameworks are required to curb private market excesses, but he probably would not suggest a reversal in the overall trend of reducing government controls and the role of public sector enterprises.

Most importantly, Carlos was realistic, pragmatic, non-doctrinaire, and aware of the wide variety of initial conditions that were in place in the developing countries as they emerged from their 19th or 20th century colonial pasts. Each was forced quickly to create an economy out of a mixture of disparate economic agents spread across more or less well-defined boundaries, and to radically alter prior patterns of transport, trade, and natural resources management. Markets were associated with the previous colonial regimes and thus unacceptable. Only governments could handle the enormous tasks facing most newly independent societies.

Even if we assume, as Carlos did, that most newly independent LDC governments are not predatory, but essentially platonic, we still must recognize that they needed not only to create a development-oriented infrastructure, but also to orchestrate a major shift in societal objectives, capturing and reallocating traditional export earnings, picking new beneficiary groups as rent recipients, building new financial institutions, restructuring education and health services, and so on. In some situations, even the basic recognition of property rights, the existence of a commercial code, and the construction of what used to be called the "preconditions" of development, were not necessarily in place. Moreover, there are usually considerable doubts with respect to the requisite availability of human resources in the private sector and the ability to take risks and perform effectively. This accentuates the tendency to look to the public sector to carry out some entrepreneurial functions as well as its customary fiscal and regulatory functions. The state is often asked not only to create the necessary infrastructure and institutions, but also to safeguard the patrimony of nature for good national purposes, to assist the working classes in their struggle against predatory foreign capitalists, to enact welfare legislation, and to shift the burden of safety nets from the family onto itself. In this way the so-called "developmentalist" state is born.

In brief, all this adds up to a rather daunting assignment for a relatively inexperienced set of politicians and bureaucrats who, for the sake of argument, have the best intentions. Moreover, there were bound to be large ingredients of euphoria and over-confidence, plus a dose of naiveté. Almost inevitably there arose the danger of the emergence of a quasi-populist package of interventions, increasingly complex and confusing over time, something we have all observed and lamented during the past several decades. Unlike the purists in the profession, however, Carlos viewed this interventionist, inward-looking phase as a virtually inevitable historical act with a legitimate role to play, including the achievement of some infant industrial sector objectives. Yet, while Carlos was as anti-colonial and anti-neocolonial as anyone, he also recognized that "guilt by association" was an inadequate reason to reject the deployment of markets on behalf of development objectives over the longer term.

Carlos was indeed an admirer of Simon Kuznets, and, in fact, in the early days of the Yale Economic Growth Center we spent many Monday afternoons together trying to determine what an ideal developing country analysis monograph might look like—something Carlos ultimately showed us in his "Essays on the Argentine Economy." What Kuznets emphasized, in relation to the role of government and markets, is the initial need for a "binding agent" or organic nationalism, i.e., "the claim of a community of feelings grounded on a common historical past and its historical heritage. (. . .) In its extreme form this represents an overriding claim for allegiance on the part of the individual members to the larger community, within certain well-defined geographic boundaries, a common language, ethnic homogeneity, cultural cohesion, a kind of cultural cement." This cement, as we are painfully aware, especially these days, is not always evident in either developing or the more developed countries. The point is, however, that to the extent that the required institutional and organizational features are not in place, the new nation-state may feel the need to create a synthetic type of nationalism. It is this feature which very much affects the size of the government's efforts relative to the use of markets during the generally interventionist early phase, creating a strong tendency to over-promise, overcommit, and under-perform. Once the precious asset of credibility is lost and rent-seeking becomes the main game in town, getting out of this box becomes increasingly difficult. The contrast between East Asia and Latin America is a case in point.

Carlos realized that the initial extent of government intervention, during the infamous import-substitution phase, was likely to differ markedly across countries and to affect habits and expectations differently. For one, the more unfavorable the initial conditions, the more likely there would be an effort to "oversell" the potential for change, leading to a widening gap between achievement and promise. At the same time, a prolonged dosage of severe import substitution was likely to affect the nature of the government itself, shifting it from the more platonic to the more predatory variety as it achieved a taste for rents and the benefits of setting its own agenda.

Carlos essentially focused his attention on the Latin American countries, most of which have a fairly plentiful natural resource endowment. Both Argentina and Colombia, the countries he worked on most intensively, could clearly afford to maintain an import-substitution regime fueled by primary exports much longer than, say, their natural resource-scarce East Asian counterparts, which were forced to shift early on towards a larger role for human capital, manufactured exports and, therefore, a necessarily larger reliance on competitive markets. Carlos recognized that markets could be mobilized as instruments for achieving post-colonial independence, but also that Latin American countries could typically afford to postpone major structural changes. This ability is undoubtedly related to their continued relative natural resource wealth, as well as their capacity to attract foreign capital virtually for the asking. Consequently, Latin America was typically subject to longer periods of import substitution, more industry-related and even firm-specific types of interventions, a fuller ossification of rent-seeking habits, and more resistance to liberalization trends—at least until the recent debt crisis changed matters.

Carlos saw marked "stop-go" policy cycles around a not very liberalizing trend as the key indicator of problems. The typical policy pattern may be described as follows: good external conditions naturally generate expansionary fiscal and monetary policies by the government; then, once the external environment deteriorates, the government makes an effort to maintain growth through continued expansionary patterns of monetary and fiscal expenditures, this time artificially substituting domestic for internationally generated purchasing power. The eventual consequence of thus delaying reality is usually a serious balance-of-payments crisis, which has to be addressed first by a return to controls and ultimately by adopting a major new liberalization package. Carlos showed convincingly, for example, that the countries that were willing and able to institute flexible exchange rate policies early on were the ones that later avoided major disasters, including the reimposition of controls followed by large scale devaluations.

With respect to the longer-term trend, Carlos noted a marked tendency to cycle back to politically convenient solutions, returning temporarily to import-substitution-like policies, favoring a rather narrow section of the (usually urban) large-scale industrial sector and, in the process, neglecting agriculture as well as medium- and small-scale industry and exports.

Carlos was always a bit skeptical about the East Asian miracle countries and the wholesale applicability of their experience to other parts of the developing world. He believed, rightly so, that the differences in initial conditions among LDCs are important in setting differential constraints on the roles of governments and markets. This has to do not only with Kuznets' pre-existing nationalism but also with country size, the wealth of the natural resource endowment, the quality of the human capital stock, and so on. Dynamically, policy options are also constrained by the initial structure of the private market and the extent of centralization or decentralization of the public sector.

Perceptions have recently changed, at least in some countries. As far as Carlos' eye could see, however, Latin American reality was one of alternating between episodes of horizontally focused interventionism and market-oriented episodes, all of which probably led to a worse development experience than would have been produced by a more consistent (if, on the average, less "good") set of policies. This gets us back to the sustainability issue, which is being recognized increasingly in the current literature. Carlos saw long ago that the sharp contrast often drawn between a decentralized, competitive market economy and a centralized, planned alternative, while useful for textbook expositions and perhaps for ideologues, is not very helpful to those who really want to understand the appropriate roles of the public and private sectors and to assist in improved policy formation. The reality often comes closer to working in the gray area, having to build on the basis of an oligopolistic, rent-seeking private sector and trying to make it more workably competitive, at the same time whittling away at centralized, elitist governments and moving them towards a more decentralized and responsive alternative. The avoidance of monopoly power in the private sector, whether emanating from multinationals or domestic firms, would therefore be a prime objective for Carlos, were he with us today. As for governments, while he did not write on this subject, I suspect he would want to disaggregate what we mean by the concept and would prefer a much larger degree of decentralization than is typically encountered.

In summary, concerning the agenda of this current volume, Carlos clearly would agree with neither Peter Timmer, who suggests we need "to get the prices right," nor with Alice Amsden, who suggests we should aim at "getting them wrong." Rather, he would wish to search for the specifics of what the World Bank now calls "market-friendly" government actions. This means locating those organizational and institutional investments, as well as those regulatory contributions of government, which will permit markets to better perform their essential coordinating and signaling functions. With time—and continued growth—Carlos would undoubtedly see the development process becoming increasingly complex, so that the lower transaction costs of unrigged markets would begin to carry relatively more weight, but always in the context of a changed, not necessarily diminished, role for government.

Carlos was also concerned with the second major topic of this book, namely the relationship between growth, distribution, and human resource development. He focused especially on the interaction between more liberal trade policies and faster growth, but he was not convinced that this would also help equity, "since most Latin American exports are from large, more capital-intensive firms." This was certainly the Colombian experience at the time he researched it, but not, I would add, the case with East Asia; in fact, along with the differential treatment of agriculture, it is one of the main reasons that the extent of complementarity between growth and income distribution has differed so sharply between Latin America and East Asia in the past.

Carlos rightly emphasized the importance of an income policy to avoid inflationary spiraling and a sensible exchange rate policy to provide an anchor. He certainly foresaw the potential importance of social contracts such as those that have been in place in Mexico during the recent period of reform. He is also one of those who recognized that egalitarianism in Latin America has often approached populism, a plea for an after-the-fact equalization of income and wealth through the redistributive fiscal and/or confiscatory powers of government, something which is much harder to reconcile with growth.

Here again, unduly misleading pronouncements and the generation of unduly high expectations have typically culminated in unusually rude awakenings. A restructuring of the way output is generated, focusing more on the minor exports of Colombia, for example, as Carlos did in his National Bureau volume, represents an alternative which clearly requires more attention. He understood well the importance of labor-intensive output and export-expansion paths for the achievement of growth with equity.

In the same general context, he also saw a problem with preferential trade arrangements within Latin America, if these were created at the expense of trade with the advanced countries. In other words, not only can trade diversion diminish the growth-enhancing effects of trade creation for a given output mix, but the composition of output may well be affected adversely—in turn affecting both growth and distribution adversely. As Andrés Velasco has pointed out, Carlos was thus fully aware of the dangers of yielding to the siren song of regional import substitution. Current unqualified enthusiasts for the burgeoning industry of regional preferential arrangements within Latin America would do well to take note of the caveats.

While Carlos approached development as an international trade economist, he also clearly saw something that has been neglected by most trade economists, including many prominent members of the current neoclassical establishment, namely that the issue of whether or not growth is consistent with equity is in large part a function of the nature of the domestic growth process. As Carlos pointed out so eloquently in his "Delinking North and South" paper, "the central point which I would emphasize is that focusing attention on trade and financial policies is wrong if one is seeking enlightenment on whether a given regime is leading its people towards equitable development. (...) The central development problems for most LDCs are internal." Internal development is indeed the dog, if you will, and the extent of export orientation is the tail, even in small countries.

Clearly, the mobilization of the interior of the economy via balanced growth between agriculture and non-agriculture, as well as via complementary rather than competitive relations between rural and urban industry, is truly a prerequisite for the successful elimination of trade-offs between growth and equity. It is a mark of the man that, while most of his writings were on the more topical dimensions of international trade, international capital movements, and the like, Carlos recognized successful development as two blades of a scissor, with labor-intensive trade requiring the complement of domestic balanced growth. The interplay between the trading and non-trading components of an economy is crucial to the overall success of the development process.

Carlos also recognized that gradual, persistent liberalization of markets at the macro level must be accompanied by microeconomic institutional reforms, concentrating in large part on the mobilization of the hinterland, both in its agricultural and non-agricultural dimensions. This requires an improved functioning of various specific intersectoral markets—including finance, labor, and commodities—as necessary complements to the invigoration of international trading activities. To accomplish this may mean focusing on the allocation of infrastructure with less bias toward urban areas, directing more technological attention to food as opposed to cash crops in agriculture, and providing better access to credit, among other things. In his standard reference work on Argentina, for example, Carlos recognized that a major cost of Peronist import-substitution policies was the retardation of the adoption of new technology in agriculture, with severe consequences for growth and the distribution of income. Overall, he evidently agreed with Irving Kravis and Elhanan Helpman, who maintained that trade remains a handmaiden of growth as much in the 20th century as much as it was in the 19th; moreover, that the right type of domestic growth, participatory and balanced, will have a great impact on trade.

Carlos also reminded us that the best domestic programs are still subject to external shocks. His work on capital inflows into Latin America in the 1920s and 1930s is highly instructive in this respect and provides fair warning for the 1990s. The main point here was that financial shocks in the advanced countries are likely to have important effects on nations at the periphery. Thus, when we congratulate ourselves today on the return to the international capital market of some of the more successful Latin American countries, e.g., Chile and Mexico, we should also note that such capital flows can quickly reverse themselves if there is a major problem external to Latin America itself. Guillermo Calvo's recent work on the return of flight capital to the region points out that low interest rates in the United States and worldwide recession among the industrial countries could easily have caused such a reversal and could reverse again. Indeed, Calvo quite explicitly sees the situation in the 1990s as following the general notion of Carlos, namely that shocks to center nations can severely affect those at the periphery, even if those who are "behaving well" in terms of their domestic policies are likely to be hurt less.

As to the role of the international financial institutions (IFIs), his work entitled "Some Economic Lessons of the Early 1980s" decried the International Monetary Fund's conditionality and encouraged a move away from issues related directly to balance of payments. I myself would find it harder to draw that line in the sand. But in his celebrated "Delinking" piece he clearly opted for the selectivity principle in building relations between North and South. This in turn leads me to believe that today he would strongly endorse the notion that the assessment of a developing country's needs and its potential to effect fundamental change, plus the policies and additional efforts required to get it there, must be in the hands of the country itself, not in those of the major creditor/donor agencies. He would also recognize that, if these conditions were met, IFI conditionality would be viewed as potentially helpful to local reformers. It is becoming increasingly evident that, in the absence of a program fully understood and "owned" by the recipient country, conditionality is likely to lack real credibility and ultimately may prove counterproductive.

Carlos served on the Kissinger Commission on Central America and dissented from its heavily political and bilateral message. He found multilateral assistance channeled through the IFIs preferable. Nevertheless, I believe he would also urge these institutions to adopt a more passive, banker-like stance, ready to respond when and if a country stands ready to propose a reform program but unwilling to force-feed it in order to meet country assistance targets. In that context, self-imposed conditionality, with the IFIs as agents, makes eminently good sense— increasingly so as the technical competence within the LDCs and IFIs converges over time.

Carlos never doubted that the international dimensions of development provided manifold opportunities for positive sum games; but he did not believe that the fair distribution of such gains would result automatically. Selective delinking internationally, like market-friendly governments internally, are seductive concepts which need fuller elucidation. Lamentably, Carlos is no longer with us to help us directly with the answers; but, to a remarkable extent, his questions and suggestions continue to guide our search.

1

The Determinants of Social Welfare

Ricardo Barros
José Márcio Camargo[1]

In this chapter we investigate the proximate determinants of the aggregate level of social welfare in Latin America. We seek to identify both the main factors that cause the level of welfare to be lower in the region when compared to the industrial economies as well as the factors that cause the level of welfare to vary across countries within the region.

The study has two important limitations that should be made explicit at the outset. First, throughout the analysis it will be assumed that the level of welfare is entirely determined by the distribution of per capita income among families, that is, the society's level of welfare becomes completely determined once the per capita income of each family in the society has been specified. No additional information is required. In other words, we exclude the independent impact of the distribution of other resources (such as public services and health) on the level of welfare.

Second, we consider only the determinants of labor income. Thus the results are more appropriate to describe the situation in urban areas than in rural areas. Moreover, the study cannot treat the specific welfare problems of the older segments of the population, such as the impact of alternative social security systems. Emphasis is on the impact of demographic composition and labor market functioning (the quality of the labor force and the quantity and quality of jobs available) on the level of welfare.

[1] The authors would like to thank Jorge Jatoba, Rosane Mendonça, Ricardo Moran, Adolfo Figueroa, and Rosemary Thorp for valuable discussions and comments on earlier versions of this paper.

To investigate the proximate determinants of the aggregate level of social welfare, we begin at the micro level by identifying the per capita income of a family as the product of a series of six factors. The six factors are: (1) the dependency ratio, (2) the proportion of adults in the family who are fully employed, (3) the bargaining power of these workers in the labor market, (4) the quality of the jobs they hold, (5) the potential quality of the labor services they can provide, and (6) the extent to which this potential quality is actually provided.

Since the welfare of the society is a function of the distribution of income among families, it can be written as a function of the joint distribution of the factors determining the level of per capita family income at the micro level. This means that the societal level of welfare depends not only on the average level of these factors, but also on how unequally they are distributed, as well as on their correlation pattern. For instance, holding the average quality constant, greater variability in the quality of machines and workers tends to reduce welfare, and this reduction is greatest when the best workers are assigned to the best machines.

In the next two sections, we develop a framework to relate the aggregate level of welfare to the joint distribution of the factors affecting the level of per capita (adult equivalent) family income. In the five subsequent sections, we use this framework to investigate the impact of six major proximate determinants of the aggregate level of welfare. In each section we gather some preliminary empirical evidence for or against the importance of each factor in determining the level of welfare in the Latin American context. Finally, in the last section we summarize our main findings and discuss some policy implications.

Social Welfare, Income Level, and Income Inequality

Consider a society with n members $(1,...,n)$ and denote by y_i the income of member i. The welfare level of this society, w, will be given by

$$w = W(y_1,...,y_n)$$

where W is the society welfare function. We are going to assume that the principles of anonymity, absence of envy, and preference for equity are satisfied. (See Shorrocks [1983] for a detailed analysis of these principles.) Under these principles the level of welfare can be written as an increasing function of (1) the average level of income and (2) the degree of equality in the distribution of income, that is,

$$w = f(\mu, L)$$

where μ denotes the average level of income and L is the Lorenz curve.[2] Since the degree of inequality declines as the Lorenz curve shifts up, the fact that f is increasing in L indicates that the level of welfare declines as the level of inequality increases.

An important class of welfare functions is the Atkinson family. A typical member of the Atkinson family is given by

$$w = \left(\sum_{i=1}^{n} (y_i)^{\epsilon} \right)^{1/\epsilon}$$

for any $\epsilon < 1$ but $\epsilon \neq 0$. When $\epsilon \to 0$ the level of welfare converges to

$$w = \sum_{i=1}^{n} \ln(y_i)$$

It can be shown that the preference for equity gets stronger as ϵ gets smaller. In fact, in the limit when $\epsilon = 1$,

$$w = \sum_{i=1}^{n} (y_i) = n \bullet \mu$$

indicating that the preference for equality disappears at this limit.

Proximate Determinants

In the previous section we briefly reviewed how the level of welfare relates to both the average level of income and the degree of income inequality. More specifically, we showed that the level of welfare is (1) an increasing function of the average income level and (2) a decreasing function of the degree of income inequality. In this section we investigate how the level of welfare relates to characteristics of the joint distribution of the proximate determinants of the level of per capita income at the micro level.

---

[2] As a matter of fact, Shorrocks (1983) demonstrates that when these three principles are satisfied, the level of welfare is an increasing function of the product μF, that is, there exists an increasing function g such that $w = g(\mu F)$. The product μF is known as the generalized Lorenz curve.

We state that a set of factors $(k_1,...,k_n)$ is the proximate determinant of the level of income, y, when they are linked by the identity

$$y \equiv \prod_{i=1}^{m} k_i$$

Several examples of identities of this type are presented in the subsequent sections.

Since the level of welfare is completely determined by the distribution of income and the distribution of income is completely determined by the joint distribution of the factors $(k_1,...,k_n)$, it follows that the level of welfare is completely determined by the joint distribution of the factors $(k_1,...,k_n)$. In this section we aim to specify more precisely how the level of welfare depends on (1) the average level of each factor k_i (2) the degree of inequality in the distribution of each of these factors, and (3) the coefficient of correlation among them.

Average level of factors. Without great loss of general applicability, and to simplify the presentation, we concentrate on the case in which there are only two proximate determinants. In this case, the average outcome can be written as

$$\mu = \mu_1 - \mu_2 \ -(1 + \rho - \nu_1 - \nu_2)$$

where μ_i and ν_i denote, respectively, the average and the coefficient of variation of factor k_i where $i=1,2$, and ρ is the coefficient of correlation between them. From this expression, it follows that higher average values for each of the factors lead to higher average incomes. Since proportional changes in the factors (which would affect the average value but not the inequality in the distribution) would have no effect on the degree of income inequality, we have established that the level of welfare is an increasing function of the average level of each factor, holding constant their degree of inequality and the degree of correlation between them.

Inequality. The impact made on the level of welfare by increments in the degree of inequality in the distribution of each factor k_i where $i=1,2$, is ambiguous. This impact is particularly sensitive to the sign of the correlation between the two factors.

On the one hand, when the two factors are positively correlated $(\rho>0)$, an increase in the degree of inequality in the distribution of one of the factors will increase the average income level (see expression (1) above) but will also increase the degree of income inequality. Therefore, the final impact on welfare will depend on the strength of society's preference for equity. For example, it can be shown that if the society has a welfare function in the Atkinson family with $\epsilon \leq 0$, increments in the inequality in the distribution of one of the factors would decrease welfare as long as $\rho > 0$. In fact, in the limit as $\epsilon \to 0$

$$w = \ln(\mu_1) + \ln(\mu_2) - L_1 - L_2$$

where L_1 and L_2 are the second Theil measure of inequality.[3] This expression indicates that increments in the inequality in the distribution of a factor reduce the level of welfare for any value of the correlation. Since the preference for equity gets stronger as ϵ gets smaller, it follows that (at least for all $\epsilon < 0$) the level of welfare is a decreasing function of the degree of inequality in the distribution of each factor.

On the other hand, when the correlation is negative, increments in the degree of inequality in the distribution of a factor will cause the average level of income to decline, but may also diminish the degree of income inequality. Hence, the result can be an increase in welfare for societies with a sufficiently strong preference for equality.

The following example should help to clarify these possibilities. Suppose, just to be specific, that the two factors are the quality of the machines and the quality of the workers. Let us assume that wages are given by the product of the quality of the worker and the quality of the machine that has been assigned to him. There are two workers of quality levels 1 and 10, respectively. The machines initially have quality levels 2 and 3. The objective is to determine the impact on the level of welfare of increasing the inequality in the machine quality such that after the transformation the quality of the machines become 1 and 4, respectively. Note that the average quality is still the same, 2.5.

Consider first the case in which the correlation is positive, so that the best worker is assigned to the best machine. In this case, the wages will initially be $30 = 3 \times 10$ and $2 = 2 \times 1$. After the transformation the wages become $40 = 4 \times 10$ and $1 = 1 \times 1$. As a result, the average income and the degree of inequality increased, leading the impact on welfare to depend on the society's taste for equality. If $\epsilon = 1/2$, $w = 47.5$ initially and $w = 53.6$ after the transformation, indicating that the society gave rela-

---

[3]

$$L(y_i, \ldots, y_n) = \ln\left(\frac{1}{n}\sum_{i=1}^{n} y_i\right) - \frac{1}{n}\sum_{i=1}^{n} \ln y_i$$

tively greater weight to the increase in average income than to the increase in income inequality. If $\epsilon = -1$, $w=1.9$ initially and $w=1.0$ after the transformation, indicating that in this case the society gave greater weight to the increase in income inequality.

Next, consider the case in which the correlation is negative so that the best worker is assigned to the worst machine. In this case the two wages will initially be $20=2\times10$ and $3=3\times1$. After the transformation the wages become $10=1\times10$ and $4=4\times1$. Hence, the average income and the degree of inequality both declined. The impact on welfare will again depend on the taste for equality. If $\epsilon = 1/2$, $w=38.5$ initially and $w=26.6$ after the transformation, indicating that the society gave greater weight to the decline in average income than to the decline in income inequality. If $\epsilon = -1$, $w=2.6$ initially and $w=2.9$ after the transformation, indicating that in this case the society gave greater weight to the decline in income inequality.

In summary, the impact on the level of welfare of increments in the degree of inequality in the distribution of a given factor is ambiguous. The level of welfare may increase or decrease depending on the nature of correlation between the factors and the strength of the preference of the society for equity.

The factors we investigate in this chapter are, in general, positively correlated. This fact is associated with the hypothesis that the society has a strong enough preference for equity ($\epsilon < 0$ if we are in the Atkinson family) to imply that greater inequality in either factor leads to lower welfare. We maintain this hypothesis implicitly throughout the subsequent sections. Hence, welfare will always be thought of as a decreasing function of the degree of inequality in each of the factors determining the level of income at the micro level.

Correlation. The impact of the degree of correlation on the level of welfare is also ambiguous. On the one hand, a higher degree of correlation between factors leads to greater average income. This is a consequence of the factors' complementary role in the production of income. In such cases, matching the best (worst) of factor 1 with the best (worst) of factor 2 will maximize total income. On the other hand, a higher degree of correlation between the two factors also leads to greater inequality in income. So, the total impact on the level of welfare will depend on the strength of the society's preference for equity.

To illustrate this ambiguity, let us reconsider our numerical example. As before, there are two workers of quality 1 and 10 and two machines of quality 2 and 3, respectively. If the correlation is positive, the best (worst) machine will be allocated to the best (worst) worker, and the wages will be 2 and 30, respectively. But, if the correlation is negative, the best (worst) machine will be allocated to the worst (best) worker, and the wages will be 3 and 20. Therefore, the average income and the degree of income inequality will both be greater in the case of positive correlation. Hence, whether or not greater correlation leads to a greater level of welfare will depend on the strength of the society's preference for equity. If $\epsilon = 1/2$, $w=47.5$ when the correlation is positive and $w=38.5$ when the correlation is negative, indicating that, in this case, the society gave greater weight to the higher average income than to the lower degree of income inequality. If $\epsilon = -1$, $w=1.9$ when the correlation is positive and $w=2.6$ when the correlation is negative, indicating that in this case the society gave greater weight to the lower degree of income inequality. More generally, it can be shown for the Atkinson family of welfare functions that increments in the degree of correlation decrease welfare if $\epsilon < 0$, and increase welfare if $\epsilon > 0$. If $\epsilon \to 0$, then the level of welfare is not influenced by the degree of correlation, since, as we have shown above, in this case

$$w = \ln(\mu_1) + \ln(\mu_2) - L_1 - L_2$$

In summary, increments in the degree of correlation increase the average level of income but also increase the degree of income inequality, with the final impact on welfare depending on the preferences of the society. In this study we assume that the society's preference for equity is strong enough so that the negative impact of a greater correlation on the degree of income equality dominates its positive impact on the level of income. Hence, we assume that a greater correlation among factors tends to decrease welfare. In the realm of the Atkinson family, this assumption is equivalent to assuming that $\epsilon < 0$.

Summary. Overall we conclude that, as long as the factors determining the level of income are positively correlated and the preference of the society for equity is strong enough, the level of welfare will be (1) increasing with the average level of each factor, (2) decreasing with the degree of inequality associated with each factor, and (3) decreasing with the degree of correlation between factors. Throughout the following sections we assume that the relationship between the level of welfare and the joint distribution of the factors determining income has these three properties.

The Dependency Ratio

Q Is the low level of social welfare in Latin America the result of insufficient income or the result of large family size?

To investigate this question it is useful to express the per adult-equivalent family income *(y)* as the product of two factors: the average income per adult in the family *(a)* and the proportion of family members who are adults *(r)*. To establish this identity formally, let *n* denote the number of persons (adult equivalents) and *m* the number of adults in the family. The income levels of each of these adults are denoted by $z_1,...,z_m$, respectively. To simplify, we assume that nonadult members do not receive any income. As a result,

$$y \equiv \frac{\sum_{j=1}^{m} z_j}{n} = \frac{\sum_{j=1}^{m} z_j}{m} \frac{m}{n} = a \bullet r = \frac{a}{1+d}$$

where

$$a \equiv \frac{\sum_{j=1}^{m} z_j}{m}$$

is the average income of the adults in the family, $r=m/n$ is the proportion of family members (in adult equivalents) who are adults, and $d=(n-m)/m$ is the dependency ratio. Hence, the aggregate level of welfare will depend on the joint distribution of *a* and *r* *(d)*. Notice that $r=1/(1+d)$, implying that *r* and *d* are inversely related.

From the discussion in the previous section, it follows that the aggregate level of welfare will be (1) increasing with the average income per adult and the average proportion of adults among family members (decreasing with the average dependency ratio), (2) decreasing with the degree of inequality in the distribution of both income per adult and proportion of adults (dependency ratio), and (3) decreasing (increasing) with the degree of correlation between income per adult and proportion of adults (dependency ratio).

The connection between the level of welfare and the mean and inequality in income per adult is considered in the subsequent sections. Hence, in this section we concentrate on the role of the distribution of families according to the dependency ratio, as well as the degree of correlation between the dependency ratio and the income per adult.

Table 1.1. Demographic Profile

Country	Fertility rate	Age structure[1]
Mexico	3.5	1.49
Guatemala	5.7	1.12
Honduras	5.5	1.13
El Salvador	4.8	1.15
Nicaragua	5.4	1.11
Costa Rica	3.2	1.64
Panama	3.1	1.65
Dominican Republic	3.7	1.50
Cuba	1.9	n/a
Venezuela	3.7	1.49
Colombia	3.1	1.67
Ecuador	4.2	1.37
Peru	4.0	1.46
Bolivia	6.0	1.21
Chile	2.7	2.05
Argentina	2.9	2.03
Paraguay	4.5	1.37
Uruguay	2.4	2.39
Brazil	3.4	1.68
Latin America	3.4	1.59
Industrial economies	1.9	3.37
World	3.5	1.82

Source: The World Bank, *World Development Report 1982.*
Note: [1]Calculated as the ratio of the percentage of population aged 15–64 years to the percentage of population aged 0–14 years.

Average. The average proportion of adults is still considerably lower in Latin America than in the industrial economies. Table 1.1 presents two relevant pieces of information. First, the table reveals that the total fertility rate in Latin America is still on the order of 3.4, almost twice the level observed in the industrial economies (1.9). Second, the table reveals that the population 15 to 64 years old in Latin America is 1.6 times the population 0 to 14 years old, approximately half the estimate for the industrial economies.

Inequality. The proportion of adults is not only lower in Latin America but is also very unequally distributed within and between countries. As far as the inequality between countries is concerned, Table 1.1 reveals that while the fertility rate in the Southern Cone (Uruguay, Argentina, and Chile) is only 50 percent higher than in the industrial economies, in Bolivia and Central America (Costa Rica and

Figure 1.1. Relationship between Total Fertility Rate and Real GDP per Capita

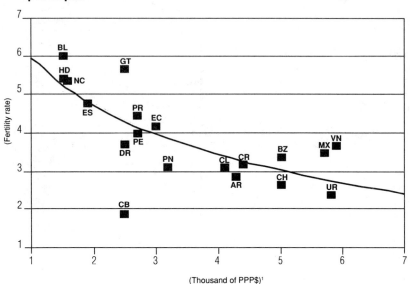

(Thousand of PPP$)[1]

Notes: [1]Purchasing Power Parity

CH	Chile	MX	Mexico
PE	Peru	VN	Venezuela
NC	Nicaragua	ES	El Salvador
BL	Bolivia	DR	Dominican Republic
HD	Honduras	CB	Cuba
GT	Guatemala	AR	Argentina
CR	Costa Rica	BZ	Brazil
UR	Uruguay	PR	Paraguay
EC	Ecuador	PN	Panama
CL	Colombia		

Panama excluded) it is more than 250 percent higher than in the industrial economies. For instance, the difference between Argentina and Bolivia (just to take two neighboring countries) is three times greater than the difference between Argentina and the industrial economies. The evidence in Table 1.1, using the age structure of the population, leads to similar results.

As far as the inequality in the proportion of adults within countries is concerned, evidence from Brazil indicates that it can be quite substantial. For instance, Merrick (1986) shows that the fertility rate varies in Brazil from 5.7 in the northeast (a value very close to the one estimated in Table 1.1 for Bolivia) to 2.7 in the State of Rio de Janeiro (a value lower than the estimate for Argentina). Moreover, he shows that the total fertility rate varies from 3 for high-income families in urban areas to 6.7 for poor families in rural areas.

Correlation. The evidence available indicates not only that the proportion of adults is quite variable, but also that most of its variability is positively correlated with income. As has been shown in the third section, this fact tends to reduce the level of welfare. With respect to the correlation between countries, Figure 1.1 indicates that the fertility rate tends to be larger in the poorest countries in Latin America and smaller in the countries with higher income, with the exception of Mexico and Venezuela. In fact, Mexico and Venezuela have relatively high levels of income for the region, but medium levels of fertility.

With respect to the correlation within countries, a strong negative correlation between adult earnings (or education) and fertility rates has been found in several studies. (See, for example, Merrick, 1986.) This correlation, however, is expected to decline very fast, as the reduction in fertility begins to reach the poor strata of the population. However, it is still true that low-income parents tend to have more children, leading to higher dependency ratios among the poor.

Capacity Utilization

Q Is the low level of social welfare in Latin America the result of low wages or a consequence of the fact that a large fraction of the adult population is not occupied, either out of the labor force or unemployed?

To address this question we express the family income per adult, a, as the product of two factors: the family income per working adult, w, and the fraction of adults who are working, u. Formally, if 1 denotes the number of working adults and only working adults have positive income, then

$$a \equiv \frac{\sum_{j=1}^{m} z_j}{m} = \frac{\sum_{j=1}^{1} z_j}{1} \frac{1}{m} = w \cdot u$$

where $u \equiv 1/m$, and

$$w \equiv \frac{\sum_{j=1}^{1} z_j}{1}.$$

For simplicity, we refer to w as the family earning capacity. In this case, u is the degree to which the family is actually using its earning capacity, so it will be referred to as capacity utilization.

Since $a = w \bullet u$, the average level and the degree of inequality in family income per adult, which partially determine the level of welfare in Latin America, are themselves a function of the joint distribution of the earning capacity, w, and the degree of capacity utilization, u.

As we showed earlier, the greater the mean and the smaller the degree of inequality in each of these two factors, the higher the level of social welfare. Moreover, any increase in the degree of correlation between these two factors will tend to reduce welfare.

Since the determinants of the level and inequality in earning capacity will be investigated in the following section, this section considers the distribution of capacity utilization and its degree of correlation with earning capacity.

Average. With respect to the average level of capacity utilization, it has been repeatedly argued that this is not an important factor in explaining low levels of income in Latin America. It has been argued that the poor in Latin America are employed, not unemployed or out of the labor force. To shed some light on this question, Table 1.2 presents three pieces of information related to the degree of utilization of the adult population in the labor market: the unemployment rate, the proportion of the adult population in the labor force, and the gender composition of the labor force.

This table reveals that although the unemployment rate is very low in the two most-populated countries in the region (Brazil and Mexico, which together account for more than 50 percent of the population in the region), on average the unemployment rate in Latin America is about the same as in Organization for Economic Cooperation and Development (OECD) economies. This table also reveals that the labor force participation rate in the region is four percentage points below the level of the industrial economies. As the last column in the table indicates, this lower participation rate for the adult population is a consequence of the lower participation of women in the labor force. Therefore, policies devoted to facilitating the participation of women in

Table 1.2. Measures of Utilization of the Adult Population in Market Activities
(Percentages)

Country	Urban rate of unemployment	Labor force participation	Women in the labor force
Mexico	4	64	31
Guatemala	13	65	26
Honduras	13	59	18
El Salvador	n/a	81	45
Nicaragua	24	67	34
Costa Rica	6	64	29
Panama	14	60	27
Dominican Republic	n/a	52	15
Cuba	n/a	n/a	32
Venezuela	10	62	22
Colombia	12	72	41
Ecuador	14	61	30
Peru	5	73	33
Bolivia	20	59	24
Chile	12	58	31
Argentina	6	62	21
Paraguay	6	81	41
Uruguay	9	62	31
Brazil	4	72	35
Latin America	6	68	32
Industrial economies	6	72	42
World	n/a	74	35

Source: The World Bank, *World Development Report 1982.*

the labor force remain important in improving welfare in Latin America. Nevertheless, we conclude that overall there is no evidence that high unemployment rates and lower labor force participation rates can explain any significant portion of the income gap between Latin America and the industrial economies.

Inequality. With respect to the variability of the unemployment and labor force participation rates, Table 1.2 indicates that there exist large differences among countries. While a few countries have very low unemployment rates (e.g., Argentina, Brazil, Costa Rica, Mexico, and Paraguay), several other countries in the region have unemployment rates between 10 percent and 15 percent (e.g., Colombia, Ecuador, Chile, Guatemala, Honduras, Panama, and Venezuela). Moreover, in two poor countries, Bolivia and Nicaragua, unemployment has recently become a serious problem. The evidence available within countries also indicates large variations in adult employment rates across families.

Figure 1.2. Relationship between Labor-force Participation and Real GDP per Capita

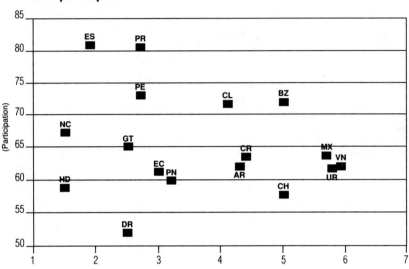

(Thousand of PPP$)

Notes:

CH	Chile	MX	Mexico
PE	Peru	VN	Venezuela
NC	Nicaragua	ES	El Salvador
BL	Bolivia	DR	Dominican Republic
HD	Honduras	CB	Cuba
GT	Guatemala	AR	Argentina
CR	Costa Rica	BZ	Brazil
UR	Uruguay	PR	Paraguay
EC	Ecuador	PN	Panama
CL	Colombia		

Correlation. The large variability of unemployment and labor force participation rates across countries may have their effects on the level of welfare attenuated by the fact that they do not seem to be strongly related to earning capacity. For instance, Figure 1.2 indicates that there exists no clear relation between the per capita income of countries and their labor force participation rate. Figure 1.3 reveals a weak but negative relationship between the unemployment rate and per capita income. However, the estimated regression line is strongly influenced by the high unem-

Figure 1.3. Relationship between Unemployment Rate and Real GDP per Capita

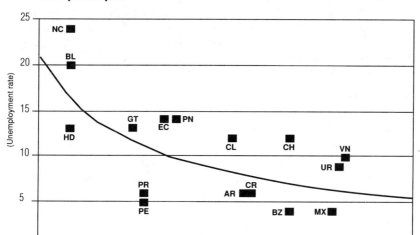

Notes:

CH	Chile	MX	Mexico
PE	Peru	VN	Venezuela
NC	Nicaragua	ES	El Salvador
BL	Bolivia	DR	Dominican Republic
HD	Honduras	CB	Cuba
GT	Guatemala	AR	Argentina
CR	Costa Rica	BZ	Brazil
UR	Uruguay	PR	Paraguay
EC	Ecuador	PN	Panama
CL	Colombia		

ployment rates in Bolivia and Nicaragua. If these two countries are removed from the regression, the negative association vanishes.

With respect to the correlation between capacity utilization (unemployment and labor force participation rates) and earning capacity within countries, there is also little evidence of a strong positive correlation. Actually, the evidence indicates that families with lower earning capacity are usually over-employed, not under-employed. (See, for example, Pastore, Zylberstajn, and Pagotto, 1983.) Moreover, there is clear evidence indicating that, following an economic downturn, household heads with low levels of education are not the ones who are affected first or the most by unemployment. The evidence suggests that secondary members (primarily youths) and household heads with intermediate levels of education (to 11 years) are those who suffer most from cyclical unemployment. (See Amadeo, Barros, Camargo, *et al.*, 1993.)

Bargaining Power

Q Is the low level of social welfare in Latin America the result of a low marginal productivity of labor or a consequence of wages being considerably below the value of workers' marginal productivity? In other words, are Latin American workers not generating much value added, or are they not receiving the value they add?

To investigate this question we define the bargaining power of workers in a given family, b, as the ratio between the average earnings of the working adults in the family, w, and the value of their marginal productivity, v. Formally, let V_j denote the value of the marginal productivity of the working adult j in the family. Therefore, the average value of the marginal productivity among working adults, v, is given by

$$v \equiv \frac{\sum_{j=1}^{1} V_j}{1}$$

and

$$b \equiv \frac{w}{v}$$

Hence, $w = b \bullet v$. Consequently, at the aggregate level welfare will depend on the joint distribution of bargaining power, b, and the value of marginal productivity, v. Increases in the average level of bargaining power or in the value of the marginal productivity will increase social welfare, whereas increases in the inequality among families with respect to either bargaining power or the value of marginal productivity will decrease social welfare. Moreover, the more positively these factors are correlated (i.e., the extent to which families with working members with greater bargaining power are those whose members have greater marginal productivity), the lower the society's level of welfare will be.

In the next section, we investigate the determinants of the value of the marginal productivity and their joint distribution. Therefore, in this section we concentrate our attention on the level and inequality in bargaining power as well as on the correlation between bargaining power and marginal productivity.

Average. We begin by considering the question of the level of the bargaining power of workers in Latin America. Overall, is the bargaining power of Latin American workers weaker than that of workers in industrial economies? Since the marginal productivity of workers is not usually observed, very few indicators are available. One possibility would be to investigate whether the degree of union activity, the degree to which labor legislation protects workers, and the proportion of the labor force covered by unions or labor legislation are smaller in Latin America than in the industrial economies. Casual evidence seems to indicate that workers are not less organized, nor the labor legislation less protective in Latin America than in Europe or North America. There seems to exist no evidence that, overall, workers in Latin America are being exploited by receiving wages well below the value of their marginal product. That is, of course, not to say that in certain isolated areas and specific sectors this phenomenon is not occurring. In summary, it is hard to believe that the overall lack of bargaining power of the laboring class could be an important factor in explaining the lower level of welfare in Latin America.

Inequality. If, on the one hand, an overall lack of bargaining power does not seem to be a problem, then, on the other hand, the distribution of power among subcategories of workers is likely to be a significant factor influencing the level of welfare. Workers' bargaining power varies widely from country to country, as well as over time. Within countries large and persistent wage differences between workers having equal observable characteristics but working in different sectors indicate that bargaining power may be quite unevenly distributed. This is a particularly useful argument to explain wage differences between public servants, workers in state enterprises, workers in the private formal sector, and workers in the private informal sector. In particular, it is still unresolved whether the lower wages of workers in the informal sector result from their weak bargaining power, which permits firms operating in this market to pay workers below the value of their marginal product, or simply because workers and jobs in this sector have lower productivity, or both.

Correlation. Even though the overall lack of bargaining power does not seem to be an important factor in Latin America, the fact that this bargaining power is heavily concentrated among skilled workers in high-paying sectors, including, in some countries, public servants, may have important consequences for the level of welfare since it implies that the bargaining power of workers and the value of their marginal product are positively correlated.

Capital Stock

Q Is the lower level of welfare in Latin America related to the scarcity of physical capital and natural resources or due to the scarcity of human resources?

To address this question, assume that firms combine capital and labor to produce goods and services. To simplify, assume that all firms have the same production function f but differ with respect to the amount of physical capital, K, they possess. Workers are heterogeneous but perfect substitutes, so the amount of labor services provided by worker i can be measured as a multiple, q_i, of the amount of labor services provided by a standard worker that is assumed, without loss of generality, to be equal to one. So, a firm with a stock of physical capital K and a labor force of n workers of quality $(q_1,...,q_n)$ will produce $f(K,L)$ where

$$L \equiv \sum_{i=1}^{n} q_i$$

Therefore, the marginal productivity of worker i, v_i, is given by

$$v_i \equiv \frac{\partial f(K,L)}{\partial L} q_i$$

To simplify, we assume that there are constant returns to scale in production. In this case,

$$\frac{\partial f(K,L)}{\partial L} = g(K/L) = g(k)$$

where $k \equiv K/L$, and

$$v_i = g(k)q_i$$

Moreover, the hypothesis of constant returns to scale also implies that the average productivity, t, is given by

$$t = \frac{f(K,L)}{L} = h(k)$$

Hence, $k = h^{-1}(t)$ and as a result

$$v_i = e(t)q_i$$

where

$$e(t) \equiv g(h^{-1}(t))$$

The above expressions for v_i show that the marginal productivity of a worker is the product of the marginal productivity of the standard worker multiplied by his or her quality level (amount of embodied human capital). Given the assumption of constant returns to scale, the marginal productivity of the standard worker in a given firm is an increasing function of the capital-labor ratio of the firm. Alternatively, the marginal productivity of the standard worker can be written as an increasing function of the average productivity. This is a useful property since estimates of average productivity are commonly available, whereas estimates of the capital-labor ratio are more difficult to obtain.

Hence, the income of the family increases with both the marginal productivity of labor in the jobs held by family members and the quality of the labor supplied by family members. Since the marginal productivity of labor depends on the capital-labor ratio, the family income will increase as the capital-labor ratio in the jobs held by family members increases. In other words, the family income will depend on both the quality of the labor services provided by the family members and the quality of the jobs in which they are employed.

At the aggregate level, welfare will depend on the joint distribution of the quality of labor and the quality of jobs. The greater the average quality of labor and the average quality of jobs, the higher the level of welfare will be. In addition, the level of welfare will also increase as the

Table 1.3. Average Productivity, Job Quality, and Worker Quality

Country	GDP (PPP) per worker	GDP (PPP) per standard worker	Workers' quality
Mexico	15.5	16.4	1.75
Guatemala	7.5	8.5	1.63
Honduras	5.0	5.8	1.59
El Salvador	4.5	5.1	1.63
Nicaragua	4.4	4.8	1.67
Costa Rica	11.6	10.9	1.96
Panama	9.0	7.7	2.17
Dominican Republic	8.3	9.3	1.67
Cuba	5.7	4.5	2.37
Venezuela	16.4	14.6	2.09
Colombia	9.5	7.8	2.26
Ecuador	8.8	8.5	1.94
Peru	6.4	5.7	2.11
Bolivia	4.8	5.6	1.61
Chile	13.7	7.8	2.35
Argentina	11.3	8.0	2.68
Paraguay	6.0	6.2	1.79
Uruguay	14.9	11.4	2.61
Brazil	11.6	13.6	1.59
Latin America	11.3	11.3	32
Industrial economies	30.7	19.6	42
World	10.3	10.5	35

Source: The World Bank, *World Development Report 1982.*

degree of inequality in the distribution of both labor and job quality is reduced. Finally, the level of welfare will decrease as the correlation between labor and job quality increases. In other words, for given marginal distributions of quality among workers and jobs, welfare will be minimized if better workers are allocated to better jobs.

The marginal distribution of the quality of labor services and of some of its determinants are investigated in the next section. In this section we concentrate on the distribution of job quality and on the correlation between job quality and labor quality.

The first column in Table 1.3 presents estimates of gross domestic product (GDP) per worker for Latin American countries and for the industrial economies as a whole. These differences, however, encompass differences in both job and worker quality. To evaluate the quality level of jobs, we need to estimate the level of productivity of labor standardized for labor quality, that is, to remove differences in labor quality. To accomplish this, first we have to construct a measure of labor quality.

To construct this measure, we assume that the quality of workers, q, increases exponentially with their number of completed years of schooling, s. Thus,

$$q = A - e^{\lambda s}$$

where A and λ are constants. Since several estimates of the relationship between wages and education indicate that wages increase exponentially with years of education, such that an extra year of education increases wages approximately 10 percent, we use $\lambda = 0.10$. Based on this expression, and assuming that q has a log-normal distribution, we obtain that the average quality of workers, $\mu(q)$, is given by

$$\mu(q) = A \bullet e^{\lambda \mu(S) + (\lambda \sigma(S))^2/2}$$

Given the average, $\mu(s)$, and the standard deviation, $\sigma(s)$, of the number of completed years of schooling for each country and region, we compute measures of the average quality of workers for each of them. These estimates are presented in the third column of Table 1.3. To arrive at these estimates we obtain the constant A by normalizing the quality of workers such that the average quality for Latin America as a whole is equal to one. Given these estimates of the average quality of workers, we obtain the average productivity per standard worker by dividing the average productivity per worker (first column) by the average quality of the labor force (third column). The results are presented in the second column of Table 1.3.

Average. The second column of Table 1.3 reveals that the average productivity of a standard worker is 75 percent greater in the industrialized economies than in Latin America.[4] Thus Table 1.3 presents evidence that lower job quality is probably the most important explanation for the lower level of welfare in Latin America as compared to the industrial economies.

Notice that the quality of jobs, as defined above, captures not only the fact that jobs in the industrial economies are more capital-intensive, but also that production in these economies is likely to be conducted more efficiently and with improved technology. Moreover, the value of the average product of Latin American workers may be simply the result of goods and services produced in Latin America being undervalued or

---

[4] However, if we compare Latin America with all economies, we find that the average quality of jobs is similar, actually even slightly higher, in Latin America.

taxed more than those produced in the industrial economies. This may be due either to discriminatory trade policies or to segmentation of the international markets, or even the inferior bargaining power of Latin American countries in international markets. In principle, the value of the average productivity could also be lower due to a lack of natural resources, but there is clear evidence that the availability of per capita arable land and energy resources is not lower in Latin America than in the industrial economies.

Furthermore, the pressure of the continuous migration of low-skilled workers from Latin American countries to industrial economies indicates that the lower quality of jobs in Latin America is certainly an important factor in explaining the lower level of welfare in the region.

Inequality. The level of welfare is a function not only of average productivity but also of its variability. The greater the variability in productivity, the lower the level of welfare will be. Table 1.3 (third column) reveals that labor productivity varies substantially across Latin American countries. Actually, the range of variation among Latin American countries is greater than between the average for the region and the average for the industrial economies. In fact, the average productivity in Brazil, Mexico, and Venezuela is 2.5 times greater than in the poor Latin American countries of Bolivia, Cuba, Paraguay, and Peru. There are also sharp differences among Latin American countries with respect to their natural resources; while some are members of OPEC, others have to import a substantial portion of their energy requirements.

Inequality in job quality within countries also tends to be very large. In fact, several sources indicate that labor markets are severely segmented in most Latin American countries. Particular attention has been given to urban-rural gaps, with several studies showing that observably equal workers tend to be more productive and receive higher wages in urban areas than in rural areas. Within rural areas the productivity of labor may also vary substantially as the distribution of land in some countries such as Brazil remains extremely concentrated. The concentration of land in the absence of a well-functioning market for credit leads small farmers to use inefficient technologies, an inadequate combination of inputs, and an inadequate choice of outputs. In this case the value of the marginal productivity of labor, land, and other inputs will vary considerably according to the size of farms.

Likewise in urban areas, several studies indicate that observably equal workers in formal activities tend to be more productive and earn more than workers in informal activities or the self-employed. Nevertheless, labor market segmentation is not restricted to the formal-

Table 1.4. Manufacturing in Brazil: Average Productivity, Job Quality, and Worker Quality

Sector	Product per std. worker[1]	Wage per std. worker[2]	Quality[3]	Years of school
Chemicals (CH)	1.5	26	1.2	5.6
Paper products (PA)	0.9	−3	1.0	4.2
Rubber products (RU)	0.2	−6	1.0	4.5
Textiles (TX)	0.6	4	1.0	4.2
Food (FO)	1.0	−13	1.0	3.9
Nonmetal products (NM)	1.0	−8	0.9	3.5
Clothing and footwear (CF)	0.6	−31	1.0	4.5
Beverages (BV)	1.0	−7	1.0	4.2
Printing and publishing (PP)	1.1	8	1.1	5.2
Wood products (WO)	0.6	−32	0.9	3.4
Furniture (FU)	0.7	−23	1.0	4.0
Leather and hides (LH)	0.6	−3	0.9	3.7
Tobacco (TO)	1.1	32	1.1	5.3
Transportation equip. (TR)	1.1	35	1.1	5.0
Metal products (MT)	2.1	18	1.0	4.6

Source: Castello Branco (1979).
Notes:
[1] Product share divided by the product of the employment share and the quality of workers (column 3).
[2] Percentage deviations from the average wage in manufacturing.
[3] See note 3 in Table 1.5 . A is now defined such that the average quality is equal to one.

informal dichotomy. As Castello Branco (1979) showed, the urban formal sector in Brazil is considerably segmented. Table 1.4, constructed from information in Castello Branco (1979), indicates that the value of the average product and the wages of workers with standard characteristics vary considerably across sectors. In fact, Table 1.4 reveals that wages for the standard worker in the high-paying sectors are more than 60 percent greater than wages in the low-paying sectors.

In summary, there is plenty of evidence that the quality of jobs or occupations varies considerably between countries, between urban and rural areas, between farms of different size, and between sectors in the urban areas. This variability leads to a lower level of social welfare than what would prevail in the case of greater homogeneity.

Correlation. The reduction in welfare caused by the inequality in job quality will be greater, the greater the correlation between the quality of jobs and the quality of workers. Hence, we next investigate the extent to which countries, regions, and sectors offering better jobs also tend to employ better educated workers.

**Figure 1.4. Relationship between Job Quality and
Years of Schooling**

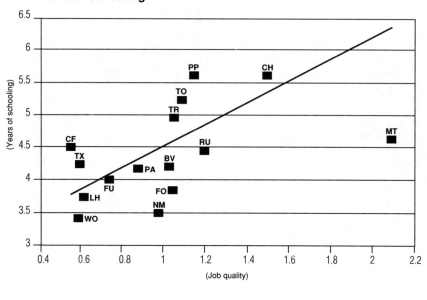

Notes:

		PP	Printing and publishing
CH	Chemicals	WO	Wood products
PA	Paper products	FU	Furniture
RU	Rubber products	LH	Leather and hides
TX	Textiles	TO	Tobacco
FO	Food	TR	Transportation equipment
NM	Nonmetal products	MT	Metal products
CF	Clothing and footwear		
BV	Beverages		

Table 1.3 indicated that there is no association across countries between job quality and worker quality. In fact, among countries with above-average job quality there is a group, including Uruguay and Venezuela, with above-average educational levels, whereas other countries with above-average job quality, such as Brazil and Mexico, have below-average educational levels. Similarly, some countries with lower job quality, such as Cuba and Peru, have above-average educational levels, while others, such as Bolivia, El Salvador, and Nicaragua, have below average educational levels. Overall, the correlation between job quality (second column of Table 1.3) and worker quality (third column of Table 1.3) is almost zero (0.05).

Within countries, however, there is strong evidence of a positive correlation between job quality and worker quality. Workers in urban areas as well as public servants tend to have better jobs and to be better educated. Finally, Figure 1.4 reveals that manufacturing sectors with higher job quality tend also to employ workers with a higher educational level.

Summary. The quality of jobs in Latin America tends to be lower than in the industrial economies. Moreover, the quality of jobs is heterogeneous, with high-quality workers matched to high-quality jobs within each country. All these characteristics help to explain the lower level of welfare prevailing in the region. However, we also showed that countries with higher job quality are not necessarily those with a better educated labor force. If the association between job quality and worker quality across countries were greater and positive, the level of welfare in Latin America would be even lower.

Incentives and Labor Quality

Q Is the lower level of welfare in Latin America the result of insufficient human capital, or is it due to the inefficiency or underutilization of available human resources?

To address this question, notice that the quality of labor services actually provided by workers, q, will generally be lower than their potential quality. In fact, when the supply of quality is costly to workers, lack of appropriate incentives or supervision may induce workers to supply labor services of a quality below their potential. Accordingly, let p denote the potential quality of workers and define the extent to which this capacity is realized by workers, f, by the ratio q/p. Thus,

$$f \equiv \frac{q}{p}$$

Therefore, $q = f \bullet p$ and, at the aggregate level, welfare will depend on the joint distribution of these two factors, f and p. Social welfare will increase as both the average potential quality and the average fraction of this potential quality actually realized increase. Moreover, welfare will decrease as the inequality in either the potential quality or the degree of utilization of this capacity increases. Finally, welfare will decrease as the correlation between workers' potential quality and the extent to which this capacity is realized increases.

Table 1.5. Indicators of Quality of Human Resources

Country	Illiteracy rate[1]	Years of mean[2]	Schooling coef. variation[3]	Life expectancy[4]
Mexico	12.7	4.7	0.89	69.7
Guatemala	44.9	4.1	0.95	63.4
Honduras	26.9	3.9	0.97	64.9
El Salvador	27.0	4.1	0.95	64.4
Nicaragua	19.0	4.3	0.93	64.8
Costa Rica	7.2	5.7	0.79	74.9
Panama	11.9	6.7	0.69	72.4
Dominican Rep.	16.7	4.3	0.93	66.7
Cuba	6.0	7.6	0.60	75.4
Venezuela	11.9	6.3	0.73	70.0
Colombia	13.3	7.1	0.65	68.8
Ecuador	14.5	5.6	0.80	66.0
Peru	14.9	6.4	0.72	63.0
Bolivia	22.5	4.0	0.96	54.5
Chile	6.6	7.5	0.61	71.8
Argentina	4.7	8.7	0.49	71.0
Paraguay	9.9	4.9	0.87	67.1
Uruguay	3.8	7.8	0.58	72.2
Brazil	18.9	3.9	0.97	65.6
Latin America	16.0	5.2	0.84	67.4
Industrial economies	2.0	10.0	0.36	74.5
World	n/a	5.0	0.86	64.7

Source: UNDP, *Human Development Report 1992*, and Ram (1990).

Notes: [1] *Human Development Report 1992* (persons aged 15 and over [1990]);

[2] *Human Development Report 1992* (persons aged 25 and over [1990]);

[3] Ram (1990);

[4] *Human Development Report 1992*. (Number of years a newborn infant would live if prevailing patterns of mortality at the time of its birth were to stay the same throughout its life.)

Average. Several characteristics of the Latin American economies are prone to generate a lack of appropriate incentives. For instance, although a heavy, direct participation of government in production could, in principle, be accomplished without generating a lack of appropriate incentives, it is doubtful that the Latin American governments could pursue this goal with enough tenacity. Therefore, the large size of government and the large degree of protectionism against foreign competition have probably generated an environment in which workers have been less likely to realize their potential than in a more competitive economy. Moreover, to the extent that the large degree of social inequality prevailing in most Latin American countries is perceived as the result of unequal access to both education and high-quality jobs, it is natural to expect that workers' incentives to supply their full potential capacity may be diminished. In summary, although it is difficult to measure the extent to which Latin American workers are underutilizing their capacity, it seems that the same labor force working in the same occupations could produce more if a more appropriate set of incentives and meritocratic rules were in place.

Although it is difficult to measure the extent to which the capacity of Latin American workers is being underutilized, the same is not true about the level of the capacity itself. Several indicators of investment in human capital clearly demonstrate that Latin American workers are less educated and less healthy than workers in the industrial economies. Table 1.5 presents three indicators of investment in human capital: illiteracy rates, average years of completed schooling, and life expectancy. In addition, the third column of Table 1.5 shows how differences in the distribution of years of completed schooling translate into differences in productivity.

Table 1.5 reveals that while 16 percent of the Latin American population 15 years of age and older is still illiterate, the corresponding proportion for the industrial economies is insignificant. The average number of years of schooling for the Latin America countries, 5.2 years, is approximately one half of the corresponding value for the industrial countries. Assuming that an extra year of education increases productivity by 10 percent, Table 1.5 suggests that the education gap between Latin America and the industrial economies implies that the average productivity in the industrial economies is approximately 60 percent greater than in Latin America. Finally, life expectancy in Latin America is approximately seven years shorter than in the industrial economies, indicating lower levels of investment in health.[5] In summary, lower labor quality is certainly among one of the main reasons for the level of welfare being lower in Latin America than in the industrial economies.

Disparity. The quality of human resources in Latin America is not only low on average but also very unequally distributed both between and within countries. In fact, as Table 1.5 reveals, the difference between Brazil and Argentina in terms of either illiteracy rates or mean years of schooling is considerably greater than between Argentina and the United

---

[5] When compared to the average for the entire world, Latin American indicators are slightly above average: life expectancy is three years longer; mean years of education is 0.2 years higher; and labor quality (productivity) is 2 percent greater (see Table 1.3).

States. In fact, the mean years of schooling in Argentina is 4.8 years higher than in Brazil but only 3.6 years lower than in the United States. Similar results hold for the illiteracy rate, which is 14 percentage points lower in Argentina than in Brazil but only 4 percentage points higher in Argentina than in the United States.

The disparity in education and health indicators is also very large within Latin American countries. As Ram (1990) has shown, the disparity in education tends to be greater in countries with average schooling level between four and seven years, which is precisely the range in most Latin American countries. A comparison between Brazil and the United States, made by Lam and Levison (1992), shows that the disparity in education in Brazil, measured by the coefficient of variation of the number of years of schooling, is almost four times the corresponding value for the United States. Table 1.5 presents estimates for the coefficient of variation of the number of years of schooling for the Latin American countries. The evidence in this table clearly indicates that disparity in education within most of Latin America is considerably greater than in the industrial economies.

The disparity of health indicators in Latin America is no less impressive than that of education. For instance, Cuba has essentially the same life expectancy as the United States, while the life expectancy in Bolivia is 20 years shorter. Differences in life expectancy within countries can also be substantial. For instance, Wood and Carvalho (1988) estimated that the life expectancy for the poor in the northeast of Brazil is 25 years shorter than for the middle class in the south of Brazil.

In summary, all indicators of the quality of human resources between and within Latin American countries indicate a very large degree of disparity. This significant disparity is another important cause of the lower level of welfare in Latin America when compared with the industrial economies.

Correlation. Finally, the impact of this extreme disparity in the quality of labor services would have an even greater negative impact on the level of welfare if potential quality were positively correlated with the intensity with which this capacity is actually realized by workers. In fact, to the extent to which the lack of appropriate incentives and motivation reach mainly workers with lower potential quality—perhaps because they are discriminated against or do not have equal access to opportunities for social progress—the effect of inequality in potential quality on the level of welfare will be even greater.

Conclusions and Policy Implications

In this study we investigate the main determinants of the aggregate level of welfare in Latin America. In the first part of the study, we show that the level of welfare is an increasing function of the average level of per capita income and a decreasing function of the degree of income inequality, provided society dislikes inequality.

We also show that average income and the degree of inequality are directly associated with the joint distribution of the factors determining the level of income. Thus, the level of welfare in a society is a function of both the level and disparity in the distribution of the factors determining income, as well as a function of the degree of correlation among them. The level of welfare is increasing with the average level of each factor and generally decreasing with the degree of inequality in the distribution of each factor.

The relationship between the level of welfare and the degree of correlation among the factors is intrinsically more complex. The level of welfare and the degree of correlation can be directly or indirectly related, depending on the strength of a society's preference for equity. To understand why, notice that when the best workers are allocated to the best machines, both average income and income disparity will be higher than when the best workers are allocated to the worst machines. Therefore, increments in the degree of correlation among the income determining factors can increase or reduce welfare, depending on whether the society judges the positive effect on the average income as greater than the negative effect on the degree of equality.

On the basis of these results, we develop a simple procedure, based on a sequence of identities, that links the per-adult equivalent family income to its various factor determinants. The entire exercise can be summarized by the following sequence of identities:

$$y = a/(1 + d)$$
$$= [1/(1 + d)] \bullet u \bullet w$$
$$= [1/(1 + d)] \bullet u \bullet b \bullet v$$
$$= [1/(1 + d)] \bullet u \bullet b \bullet g(k) \bullet q$$
$$= [1/(1 + d)] \bullet u \bullet b \bullet g(k) \bullet p \bullet f$$

where:

y = per-adult equivalent family income
a = average income of adults
d = family dependency ratio
u = family earnings capacity utilization

w = family earnings capacity
b = bargaining power of workers in a given family
v = value of marginal productivity
k = capital-labor ratio
q = quality of labor services
f = fraction of the potential quality actually used
p = potential quality of workers
g = marginal productivity function

This last expression states that the income level of a given family increases with the family dependency ratio and increases with (1) the degree of utilization of the earnings capacity of the family, (2) the bargaining power of their working members, (3) the quality of the jobs they hold, (4) the quality of the labor services they can provide, and (5) the extent to which they actually supply the quality of services of which they are capable.

Some of these factors, such as the bargaining power of workers and the extent to which they are actually supplying the potential quality of services they are capable of, are difficult to quantify. Other factors, however, such as the dependency ratio and the quality of labor, are easier to quantify.

Next we analyze to what extent each of these determinants of income can explain disparities in welfare among Latin America countries and between these countries and the industrial economies. To accomplish this goal we investigate the average level and the degree of inequality in each factor, as well as their correlation patterns. The degree of inequality in the distribution of each factor and the correlation among them were investigated both within countries and across countries. Let us now summarize the main results.

First of all, there is a wide range of variation among the income determining factors within each country and among Latin American countries. Fertility rates, for example, vary from 6 in Bolivia to 1.9 in Cuba, while the average for the region is 3.4. The open unemployment rate is 24 percent of the labor force in Nicaragua as compared to 4 percent in Brazil and Mexico, with the average open unemployment rate for the region as low as 6 percent. The purchasing power parity (PPP) index of GDP per standard worker, which is a measure of the quality of the jobs offered in each country, varies from 4.5 in Cuba to 16.4 in Mexico, with 11.3 being the average for Latin America. The index of worker quality varies from 0.86 in Brazil and Honduras to 1.41 in Argentina, with the average for the region, by construction, at 1.

Although such information is much more difficult to obtain, we also try to present evidence on the degree of variation of some these factors within each of the Latin American countries. In all cases in which evidence was available, the degree of inequality was shown to be very high (see Table 1.5, for example).

Another important finding is that the degree of correlation among some of these factors is not very high. To take just one example, Brazil and Mexico are among those countries with the highest index of job quality in the region, but their indexes of labor quality are well below average. Argentina, on the other hand, has the more qualified labor force and relatively low job quality. The relatively low correlation between job quality and labor quality reduces both the average per capita income for the region and the degree of income inequality. The first effect reduces welfare, while the second increases welfare, with the second effect dominating when the society's preference for equity is strong enough.

There is still considerable research to be done to determine the relative importance of these factors in affecting overall levels of inequality, poverty, and welfare. The main objective of this study was to identify these factors and to provide some very preliminary indications of their relative importance.

Next, we use a simplification of the analysis to summarize some of its main findings and to identify which set of factors is of greatest importance in explaining the differences in welfare among Latin American countries and between Latin America and the industrial economies. To do so, it is convenient to assume the production function is of the Cobb-Douglas type. In this case, the last equation (above) becomes:

$$y = (1-\alpha) \bullet r \bullet u \bullet \delta \bullet q$$

where α is the parameter of the Cobb-Douglas production function and $\delta \equiv f(k) \bullet b$ is the value of the average productivity.

For the sake of simplicity we will ignore the level of inequality of each of the factors. This means that the following comparisons take into account only the average level of the factors, not their distribution or the correlation between them, which, as we have shown, is also of great importance in determining the level of welfare and poverty.

Given these simplifying assumptions and the above expression for y, we can write the ratio of the average GDP per capita, γ, for two regions or countries (i and j) which are being compared as

$$\gamma = (1 + \beta_r) \bullet (1 + \beta u) \bullet (1 + \beta \delta) \bullet (1 + \beta_q)$$

where

$$\gamma \equiv y_i / y_j$$

and

$$1 + \beta_f \equiv f_i / f_j$$

for $f=r, u, \delta, q$.

Large values of β_f indicate that the factor f is important in explaining differences in welfare. Table 1.6 presents the average values of the factors r, u, δ, and q for Latin American countries, the industrialized economies, all economies in the world, and for the poorest (Bolivia) and the richest (Uruguay) Latin American countries. The second panel of Table 1.6 presents the values of $(\beta_f : f=r,u,\delta,q)$ for several comparisons between regions and countries.

The most important result that appears in this table is that labor quality and job quality are the two most important factors in explaining differences between Latin American countries and industrial economies, as well as between rich and poor countries within Latin America. The other two factors considered, the proportion of adults in the population and the capacity utilization (labor force as a fraction of the adult population), are much less important in explaining these differences. They also penalize the poor countries and regions, but to a much smaller extent.

The proportion of adults in Latin America is equal to the average for all countries but 10 percent lower than in the industrial economies. The poorest country in Latin America, Bolivia, has a proportion of adults 20 percent lower than the richest country, Uruguay. Similar results are obtained for capacity utilization. On the other hand, labor quality is 60 percent higher in the industrial economies than in Latin America. The difference between Uruguay and Bolivia is also substantial—40 percent. Job quality is also much higher in the industrial economies than in Latin America (70 percent higher) and in Uruguay as compared to Bolivia (100 percent). Note that this index includes not only the quality of jobs but also the capacity of workers to earn their marginal product (or more), that is, their bargaining power.

Policy implications based on these results follow. First of all, although policies to reduce the rate of growth of population cannot be considered unimportant, they alone will not be sufficient to improve the level of welfare in the region significantly. Secondly, unemployment is an important factor that reduces welfare in Latin America as com-

Table 1.6. Proximate Determinants of Poverty: A Simplified Approach

	d	u	p	q
Latin America	59	68	11.3	1.0
Uruguay	63	62	11.4	1.3
Bolivia	53	59	5.6	0.9
Industrial economies	67	73	19.6	1.6
World	61	74	10.5	1.0
Industrial economies versus Latin America	1.1	1.1	1.7	1.6
World versus Latin America	1.0	1.1	0.9	1.0
Uruguay versus Bolivia	1.2	1.1	2.0	1.4

Source: World Bank, World Development Report 1982.

pared to the developed world, but again, except for specific countries, it is not the main generator of poverty and of low welfare in the region. Thus, employment creation as well as birth control policies should be considered auxiliary policies to reduce poverty and increase welfare in Latin America. For these policies to have an important impact on poverty and welfare, they should be accompanied by other instruments that increase both the quality of the labor force and the quality of jobs in the region.

Policies that improve the quality of the labor force or the extent to which the labor force is capable of supplying its potential labor power are of great importance. Policies that increase human capital investment are certainly among them. Thus, to improve the quality of the educational system and to reduce the opportunity costs for the children of poor families to stay in school should be considered important instruments for reducing poverty and increasing welfare. Note, however, that, as emphasized by Amadeo, et al. (1993), some policies (like those that increase the time families and children have to dedicate to education) improve the quality of the education but also increase the cost of being in school, possibly leading to reductions in school attendance among poor children. As a result, these policies can increase the disparity in the distribution of human capital in the country, adversely affecting poverty and welfare. Thus, educational policies devoted to increasing the quality of the labor force should be designed to reduce the total costs and increase the total benefits of children being in school. (See Amadeo, *et al.,* 1993, for an extensive discussion of this question.) Examples of such policies are free and better transportation, free and better school books and materials, better prepared teachers, and so on.

The distribution of human capital is as important or perhaps even more important than the level of human capital in reducing poverty and increasing welfare in Latin America. If that is so, since poor children are mainly concentrated at the primary education level and seldom reach higher levels, to concentrate public resources on improving the quality of primary education can be a very effective instrument for reducing the inequality in the distribution of human capital and thus reducing poverty and increasing welfare.

On the other hand, reducing the cost of being in school can be a powerful instrument for increasing human capital accumulation by the poor. When the family is very poor, the income it loses by keeping children in school is very significant. Therefore, the result can be a high early drop-out rate. In this case, income transfer to very poor families to compensate for the opportunity cost of sending their children to school can be an effective way of increasing human capital accumulation by the poor and improving the average quality of the labor force, while at the same time reducing inequality.

Another important set of policies for improving the quality of the labor force is related to the incentives provided by the institutional framework that determines the structure of labor contracts. This directly affects both the extent to which firms and workers invest in human capital accumulation (and thus the quality of the labor force) and the extent to which workers will provide their full potential labor power. There are three sets of institutions that are of great importance in this context. First, institutions that provide incentives for workers and firms to emphasize short-run labor relations tend to reduce investment in training by firms and thus the quality of the labor force, since investments in training are embodied in workers and cannot be appropriated by firms.

Second, institutions that are unable to generate peaceful relations between management and labor also tend to reduce the quality of the labor force.

Finally, institutions that create incentives for workers to increase their effort and productivity (such as payment schemes based on individual performance) can also serve as very important instruments for improving labor force quality and thus reduce poverty and increase welfare.

Policies aimed at increasing job quality are also of great importance for improving the welfare of workers. These are policies directed at increasing the quality of the jobs, per se, as well as the bargaining power of workers. Since the quality of jobs is directly related to the amount of physical capital available in the job, policies that induce increases in the rate of investment are important instruments for reducing poverty and increasing welfare.

Policies aimed at increasing workers' bargaining power can also increase welfare and reduce poverty. It is important to avoid those institutional frameworks that not only increase the average bargaining power of workers but also increase inequality. Centralization of some aspects of the collective bargaining process is one example. However, a rigid centralization of collective bargaining can also generate labor market rigidities that can increase unemployment and should therefore be considered with care.

References

Amadeo, E., R. Barros, J.M. Camargo, *et al.* 1993. Human Resources in the Adjustment Process. Instituto de Pesquisa Econômica Aplicada, Rio de Janeiro. Mimeo.

Atkinson, A.B. 1970. On the Measurement of Inequality. *Journal of Economic Theory* 2:244–263.

Castello Branco, R., 1979. Crescimento Acelerado e o Mercado de Trabalho: a experiência brasileira. *Série Teses N.1.* Rio de Janeiro: Fundação Getúlio Vargas.

Lam, D., and D. Levison. 1992. Age, Experience and Schooling: Decomposing Earnings Inequality in the United States and Brazil. *Sociological Inquiry* 62 (2).

Merrick, T.W. 1986. A População Brasileira a partir de 1945. In *A Transicão Incompleta,* eds. Edmar Bacha and Herbert S. Klein. Rio de Janeiro: Paz e Terra.

Pastore, José, Hélio Zylberstajn, and Carmen Silva Pagotto. 1983. *Mudança Social e Pobreza no Brasil: 1970–1980 (O que ocorreu com a família brasileira?).* São Paulo: Pioneira/FIPE.

Ram, R. 1990. Educational Expansion and Schooling Inequality: International Evidence and Some Implications. *The Review of Economics and Statistics* 72 (2):266–74.

Shorrocks, A.F. 1983. Ranking Income Distributions. *Econometrica* 50 (197):3–17.

United Nations Development Programme (UNDP). 1992. *Human Development Report 1992.* New York: Oxford University Press.

Wood, C.H., and J.A.M. Carvalho. 1988. *The Demography of Inequality in Brazil.* Cambridge: Cambridge University Press.

The World Bank. 1982. *World Development Report 1982.* New York: Oxford University Press.

Comment

Adolfo Figueroa
Catholic University of Peru, Lima

Barros and Camargo attempt to explain both the levels and the inequality of income in Latin America, using individual earnings as a starting point. This income is broken down into a series of factors based on a sequence of identities. From these identities, the authors expect to derive the determinants of income levels and inequality in the economies of the region.

Methodology

The identities are based on the labor income of the individual, whose income is first broken down into the dependency ratio and labor income of the adults in the family. The latter is then broken down into the degree of capacity utilization of labor and the earnings capacity of the adults. The latter is, in turn, broken down into the bargaining power of the worker and the value of the marginal productivity of labor. Marginal labor productivity is then further separated into the marginal productivity of the standard worker and the quality of labor. Finally, labor quality is broken down into the potential quality of labor and the proportion of the potential quality of labor actually realized.

This particular sequence of identities has two problems. First, the system is based on labor incomes alone, which means that incomes from rents and profits are ignored. This is unwarranted since some 30 percent to 40 percent of national income, depending on the country, is distributed in those forms in Latin America. The evidence they show throughout the paper, however, is total income. If the authors' intention was to deal only with the poor groups in each country, whose income is clearly based largely on their labor, the entire paper would need to be reworked.

Second, to assume both a degree of bargaining power and the equality between wages and the value of the marginal product of labor is logically inconsistent. If the worker is going to get his marginal product, the market structure must be one of perfect competition. We assume either bargaining power or wages to be equal to marginal product, but not both.

Empirical Evidence

The authors present some interesting demographic comparisons. The dependency rate is considerably higher in Latin America than in the industrial economies. The labor force participation rate is a little lower, but among women it is remarkably lower. Why is participation of women in the labor force lower? The open unemployment rate in Latin America is, on average, about the same as in the OECD countries. Therefore, the authors conclude that open unemployment and labor participation cannot explain the gap between Latin America and the industrial economies.

Looking at the variables related to the production process, this chapter also presents some evidence to support the argument that lower job quality is probably the most important explanation for the lower income level in Latin America compared to the industrial countries. This is another way of saying that industrial economies are more intensive in capital. Also, lower labor quality is another important reason for the gap between Latin America and the industrial countries.

The study also shows that among Latin American countries there exists a large diversity of situations, as reflected in the variables examined. The distribution by country of some of the explanatory variables shows a high degree of consistency with the hypotheses of the study.

By introducing some assumptions, such as that wages are equal to the marginal product of labor, that workers supply everything they can in terms of the potential quality of labor services, and that a Cobb-Douglas production function is obtained, the authors arrive at the conclusion that "[t]he most important result. . .is that labor quality and job quality are the two most important factors in explaining differences between Latin American countries and industrial economies, as well as between rich and poor countries within Latin America. The other two factors considered, the proportion of adults in the population and the capacity utilization... are much less important in explaining these differences" (page 32).

Contribution

The authors' basic conclusion seems consistent with the current conventional wisdom on development economics. Human resources or human capital are now considered one of the fundamental factors of economic growth. The authors' policy recommendations are derived from this basic finding: policy instruments should be directed toward increasing the quality of the labor force and the quality of jobs. But this is the most one can conclude from a sequence of identities. What are the factors that explain the development of human capital? Which are the exogenous variables of the system from which policy instruments may be drawn? No answer to these questions can be found in the paper. Identities do not yield casual relationships.

Despite the promises made by the authors at the beginning of the chapter, the question of income distribution within a country has been neglected. Hence, all the discussion presented in the introductory section on social welfare becomes redundant. Actually, the income-level analysis is done in terms of the "representative agent" (an individual receiving only labor income). This is nowadays a very common method of analysis in macroeconomics, but it has lately been subject to severe criticism on theoretical grounds.[1] In the case of an analysis of income distribution, the use of the representative agent seems even more questionable. It is not surprising, therefore, that the authors were not able to deal with their subject in a satisfactory fashion.

The use of identities certainly has some merit, but also some limits. Identities can help us in identifying the sources of variation of a variable, but they cannot give us an explanation. That is, they cannot show causal relationships; only theory can do this. There is an analogy with the well-known discussion in macroeconomics in which the "quantity equation of money" ($MV=PQ$) has been used *ad nauseam* to "understand" the causes of inflation. Today, it is clear that we were asking too much of this equation. Theory has taken over.

The authors have contributed to our understanding of development in Latin America by extracting some interesting suggestions out of a sequence of identities. However, real progress will come only when theory (and the corresponding necessary empirical evidence) are developed to permit us to understand the process by which a capitalist economy remains relatively poor and inegalitarian. For instance, the authors' results suggest that an analysis of the workings of labor markets may be crucial for understanding income levels and inequality in Latin America. This is indeed an area in which our level of ignorance seems very high and more research is badly needed.

Comment

Rosemary Thorp

The principal "roots" considered concern family size, quality of work, quality of labor, and extent of use of earnings capacity. The authors make it clear that they are addressing only the proximate determinants of "the roots of poverty." The core of the empirical work is a comparison of Latin America and the industrialized countries, though there also is considerable documentation of the variation between and within countries.

---

[1] See Alan P. Kirman, 1992, Whom or What Does the Representative Individual Represent? *Journal of Economic Perspectives* 6: 2.

The final version we have here includes a new and useful section on policy implications.

The chapter is written with great clarity. It concentrates on the precise formulation of questions and succeeds in delineating the significance of interactions between the different factors being considered as explanations of poverty and inequality. My comments that follow first make some suggestions as to the validity and interpretation of the analysis itself and, second, address the issues of causality and policy conclusions.

Taking the analysis within its own terms I would like to discuss the issues of the valuation of workers' productivity, bargaining power, unemployment, and education. On productivity, the discussion on pages 18–19 seems to me to be of pivotal importance in the search for roots. The point is made there that using the market value of the product of a worker to indicate "the quality of the job" implies an acceptance of that market valuation, which may not be appropriate. Between countries, it is pointed out that market prices may reflect unequal bargaining power, discriminatory trade policies, or segmentation of the international market. Within countries, market segmentation resulting from the prior unequal distribution of wealth is emphasized. These points are fundamental to an analysis of the "roots" of poverty and deserve much deeper exploration. It is not only the prior unequal distribution of resources that segments markets, but also power structures exploiting gender, race, and class differences. This area is so important that a framework that introduces them as a qualification to the analysis, then drops them in the final synthesis and conclusion, leaves me unsatisfied.

The authors' treatment of workers' bargaining power raises a similar question. They concluded that it was not a significant element in the overall explanation of poverty, though important when comparing subgroups, on the grounds that levels of worker organization are comparable in the industrialized countries and in Latin America. But while workers may be organized, they may still be unable to protect themselves—witness the drastic cuts in real wages of the 1980s. (What cutting formal sector wages does to inequality when the formal sector is as small as it is in, say, Peru, is a separate issue.) The general point is that workers' inability to realize the value of their marginal product, in the face of monopoly structures and barriers of class, race, gender, and previous resource endowment, is a major explanation of poverty, rather than a qualification to be recognized and then put aside.

The third point, the unemployment rate, leads me to a different concern, the need to be cautious about data. The evidence of quite high open unemployment in a number of Latin American countries is taken as grounds for concluding that we have too easily given credence to the idea that quality of employment, not quantity, is the problem. But I would need much more convincing that the data are meaningful; given the way the unemployment figures are created, it is perfectly possible and, I suspect, probable that people who declare themselves unemployed in fact have a range of informal or illegal jobs. It is an increasingly common phenomenon in the industrialized countries, after all. This takes us straight back to the issue of job quality.

The data we have to work with are also the source of my concern over "worker quality," which is assessed by the conventional variable of years of schooling. This omits numerous areas from the analysis of the roots of poverty, such as the possible inappropriateness of formal schooling, the relevance of experience, and the need for training in more specific skills. It is not plausible that the authors could have solved these problems, but due caution, at least, is in order.

Taking into account these points, however, simply reinforces the authors' final conclusion (which is no doubt their defense), since they underline the roles of job and worker quality. I am, however, concerned about the conclusion in another sense, and this brings me to my second line of comment: the size of the ratio of the values of the variables in Table 1.6 for industrialized and Latin American countries is taken as a straightforward indication of the strength of their impact on poverty. But this conclusion depends on simplifying the assumptions that have to be made in their final section to reach the simple comparison, namely all those necessary to apply a Cobb-Douglas function. The analysis thus leaves aside the earlier interesting discussion exploring the extent to which actual and potential worker quality may diverge, as well as the whole issue of bargaining power. This is worrisome, since the principal policy conclusion is drawn on the basis of this table; population and employment policies are apparently seen as relatively unimportant as a means for attacking poverty.

Surely the policy discussion should be quite radically qualified, not only for this reason, but also because the authors are discussing only proximate causes. If, for example, power structures are seen as fundamental determinants, this would color our evaluation of their menu of policy suggestions.

In conclusion, both my lines of comment lead me in the same direction. If we are anxious to pursue the roots of poverty, we need to encourage the authors to take as the next stage of their work a framework that gets closer to identifying such roots. My own bias, based on the evidence provided by detailed case studies, is to suggest that we need to examine twin cases with significant variations in the factors determining both access to resources and the distribution of the benefits from work.

2

Growth, Distribution, and Human Resources

François Bourguignon[1]

Between 1960 and 1985, GDP per capita in Latin American countries grew at an average annual rate that was 2.5 percent below that of Asian countries (excluding the Indian peninsula). In 1960, GDP per capita was 70 percent higher in Latin America than in Asia; by 1985, that figure had become negative. It is true that the share of physical investment in GDP has been, on average, 5 percent to 6 percent lower in Latin America over the whole period. Yet investments in human capital as described by primary and secondary school enrollment rates were comparable in the two regions (see Table 2.1). If the difference in growth achievements had to be explained solely by differences in physical investment, it would be necessary to assume a marginal overall return of capital close to 50 percent to explain the gap between Latin America and Asia. As such a figure is quite implausible, some specific factors must be found to explain the relatively poor growth performance of Latin American countries since 1960.

The main hypothesis analyzed in this chapter is that economic growth in Latin America is negatively affected by the comparatively high inequality in the distribution of productive assets and personal incomes. Carlos Díaz-Alejandro has repeatedly insisted upon the importance of income inequality for understanding Latin American idiosyncrasies, especially those relating to phenomena of the political economy. Here, we take a more reduced-form view by investigating the structural-empirical relationship between growth and inequality within a cross-section of developing countries and examining some Latin American singularities.

[1] The author wishes to thank participants at the conference, in particular Nora Lustig and Andres Velasco, for useful comments on an earlier version.

Table 2.1. Regional Indicators of Growth, Distribution, Educational Development, and Trade Protection
(Arithmetic means on a sample of 35 developing countries)[a]

Region	Asia	Latin America	Africa	Total
1960 Real GDP per capita (1985 US$)[b]	1462	2468	1023	1583
1970 Real GDP per capita (1985 US$)[b]	2272	3141	1396	2198
Growth of real GDP per capita (%):				
1960–85	3.9	1.5	1.4	2.3
Growth of real GDP per capita (%):				
1970–85	3.7	.6	.5	1.7
Share of investment in GDP				
(average 1960–85, %)	21.3	15.2	16.2	17.8
Primary school enrollment[c] (%): 1960	78.7	91.7	55.1	73.8
1970	92.8	99.9	74.3	88.1
Secondary school enrollment[c] (%): 1960	20.8	21.0	3.8	14.7
1970	36.0	32.5	9.9	25.6
Income distribution (%) (1970)[d]				
Share of bottom 40%	12.5	9.9	11.0	11.3
Share of bottom 60%	25.8	21.4	22.1	23.2
Share of top 20%	53.2	59.8	59.8	57.4
Land distribution (%) (1970)				
Share of small and medium farmers	88.4	45.7	79.5	73.3
Trade protection[e]	45.0	83.0	0.0	50.0

[a] The list of countries includes Algeria, Argentina, Chile, Colombia, Congo, Costa Rica, Côte d'Ivoire, Egypt, El Salvador, Gabon, Honduras, Hong Kong, Iran, Kenya, Korea, Malawi, Malaysia, Morocco, Panama, Peru, Philippines, Senegal, Sierra Leone, South Africa, Spain, Sri Lanka, Sudan, Taiwan, Tanzania, Thailand, Togo, Uruguay, Venezuela, Yugoslavia, Zambia, Zimbabwe.
[b] Corrected by ppp figures.
[c] *World Development Report 1990*, World Bank.
[d] Bourguignon and Morrisson (1990).
[e] National dummy variables taken from Bourguignon and Morrisson (1990).

More precisely, this chapter is a follow-up on previous work in which we sought to integrate two different streams of the empirical cross-sectional development literature: the determinants of growth and those of income distribution. This is done with a general theoretical framework in which growth, income distribution, and changes in income distribution are mutually dependent and appear to be determined simultaneously by initial factor endowments, their distribution in the population, market distortions, and changes in these three sets of variables. In such a framework, it indeed appears possible that an unequal initial distribution of factor endowments is a deterrent to growth and the cause of persistent inequalities, despite a reasonably high rate of investment in human resources.

The relationship between growth and distribution has a rather long tradition in economics. It must be stressed, however, that the approach followed in this study departs from the voluminous empirical and theoretical literature inspired by the well-known Kuznets hypothesis, according to which income inequality along the growth path of a given country might increase at first and then decrease with the level of income. Here, what matters is the growth rate of per capita income, rather than its level. From that point of view, this chapter is along the lines of recent work by Alesina and Rodrik (1991), Persson and Tabellini (1992), and others, in which income distribution determines investment and growth through various mechanisms of the political economy. A positive association between the equality in (primary) incomes and growth is expected because the political economy equilibrium or the voting system in democracies requires fewer inequality-correcting measures, and, therefore, fewer distortions are created that may reduce the accumulation of productive factors.[2]

Such an inverse relationship betwen inequality and per capita GDP growth was actually demonstrated in a cross-section of countries by the authors mentioned in the preceding paragraph. Persson and Tabellini (1991 and 1992), for instance, show that growth is faster in countries with more equal land distribution and in countries with more equal income distribution, when the sample is restricted to democracies. However, cross-sectional analyses of this sort are subject to several ambiguities, which can be resolved only through the specification of a full structural model and a proper handling of possible simultaneity biases. The model estimated in this chapter through a sample of developing countries leads to several qualifications of previous results. It also offers a more complete analysis of the way income distribution affects growth—whether directly or through the accumulation of physical and human capital—and stresses regional singularities.

The first part of this chapter is devoted to a short analysis of the theoretical structure of the complex relationship between growth, income distribution, human resources, and other factor accumulation in a neoclassical framework. Some formalization is used for ease of presentation, but the argument is, in fact, quite general and simple. The objective is to grasp the various channels through which the phenomena under study interact, rather than to investigate the resulting direction of these various interactions. The second part examines the empirical cross-sectional evidence on these interactions contained in a sample of 36 developing countries, of

---

[2] Saint-Paul and Verdier (1991) make the point that growth may be faster in inegalitarian economies if the correction of inequalities goes through public education.

which 10 are in Latin America. This is done using as a starting point the recent work on cross-sectional determinants of growth, particularly the work of Mankiw, Romer, and Weil (1992), on the one hand, and some previous work relating to the Kuznets curve, on the other.[3] In a second step, we integrate both types of analysis within the more general simultaneous framework identified in the first part of the paper. The lessons to be learned from that exercise in general, and for the understanding of Latin American growth in particular, are discussed in the concluding section.

Growth and Distribution: A Theoretical Framework

In this section we analyze the nature of the relationship between growth, factor accumulation, and income distribution. We begin with the general determinants of income distribution in a static economy. We then extend the analysis to a dynamic framework. Finally, we discuss some general long-term equilibrium properties of that model.

A Reduced-form Model of Income Distribution

Before considering growth issues, let us take a static point of view to describe the determinants of income distribution at some given stage of development.[4] To simplify, we assume that all goods are tradeable so that domestic (relative) prices are international prices corrected by tariff duties. We also assume that production uses several factors (j) that are available in quantities F_j in the economy. We know from international trade theory that, under these conditions, the sectoral structure of production and the remuneration rates of productive factors depend on factor endowments (F), international prices (p), and tariff duties (t) (or, more generally, trade barriers and domestic indirect taxation). Denoting by q the vector of outputs, and by w the vector of factor remuneration rates, the standard small economy model thus implies the following reduced-form model for production and factor rewards:

$$q = G(F, p, t) \tag{1}$$

$$w = H(F, p, t) \tag{2}$$

The specific properties of these functions do not matter for the moment.

---

[3] There are various surveys of the empirical literature on the Kuznets curve. See for instance Anand and Kanbur (1985).

[4] This section relies on Bourguignon and Morrisson (1990).

In order to model the distribution of incomes, we assume that an individual i in the population owns an amount $F_{ji} = a_{ji}.F_j$ of factor j. The matrix (a_{ij}) thus describes the structure of property in the economy. Of course, empirical relevance requires that factors be defined with enough detail: labor of different types (human capital), land with different characteristics, physical capital in various firms or sectors, etc. Given the factors' remuneration rates, w, the primary income[5] of individual i is simply defined as:

$$y_i = \Sigma \, F_{ji} \bullet w_j \qquad (3)$$

With that definition, the distribution of incomes—that is, the set of individual incomes $\Upsilon = (y_1, y_2,...)$—appears as a function of the property structure of the various factors in the economy (i.e., the whole matrix (a); the factor endowments (F); and, through the remuneration rates, the set of international prices (p); and tariff duties (t)). A reduced form for the income distribution is thus:

$$Y = D(F, a, p, t) \qquad (4)$$

A few examples may help to understand the meaning of that expression. Suppose that factor 1 is land and that its distribution in the population is uncorrelated with that of other factors. Then an increase in the concentration of land ownership should, other things being equal, increase the inequality of income distribution. On the other hand, an increase in the availability of land, without a change in its distribution, has an ambiguous effect on the distribution of incomes. If its concentration is higher than that of other factors, then inequality should increase. However, if there is more land relative to other factors, then its remuneration rate must fall. Its share of GDP could possibly fall as well, depending on the overall elasticity of substitution between land and the other factors. The latter phenomenon may well compensate for the former. Even if land is more unequally distributed than other factors, an increase in its relative supply might eventually reduce the degree of inequality of income distribution. Note though that such a conclusion depends crucially not only on the elasticity of substitution across factors but also on the correlation between their distribution. If land ownership is highly correlated with that of physical capital, and if land is substitutable mostly with that same factor, then a change in the

---

[5] Thus ignoring all income redistribution mechanisms.

availability of land might have a limited overall impact on income distribution.

One may assume that all countries face the same set of international prices. If, in addition, they have the same sectoral production functions, and if all goods are indeed tradeable, then equation (4) provides the basis for a cross-sectional analysis of the determinants of income inequality.[6]

It may be noted that the exogeneity of the vector t of tariff duties, indirect taxes, and other government interventions that lead to market distortions in the economy may be questionable. As in the work surveyed by Persson and Tabellini (1992), one may consider that these variables are determined by some political economy equilibrium that depends on the inequality of the primary distribution of income. With equal international prices across countries, the arguments of the reduced form model (4) would then simply be F and a.

A Reduced-form Model for Growth

Aggregating the supply functions in expression (1) through the price system p—possibly corrected by the market distortion factors, t—yields an expression of the type:

$$GDP = Q(F, p, t) \qquad (5)$$

Differentiating with respect to time leads to the fundamental dynamic relationship:

$$g = \Sigma\, \alpha_j \delta F_j + TP + [\Sigma\, \beta_i\, \delta p_i + \Sigma \gamma_i\, \delta t_i)] \qquad (6)$$

where g is the aggregate rate of growth of the economy; α_j, β_i, and γ_i are obtained from the partial derivatives of the function Q in expression (5); and δx stands for the rate of change of variable x. TP stands for technical progress and corresponds to the direct exogenous effect of time on aggregate output.

Expression (6) is the standard formula for growth accounting. Aggregate growth appears first as a combination of the growth rates of

---

[6] Note that specialization may cause cross-country differences in the form of the function $D( )$. Also, it must be stressed that expression (4) remains valid for an economy with non-tradeable goods. The income distribution Y then also enters in the determination of factor remuneration rates. But the reduced-form (4) remains valid, with p referring then to the subset of tradeable goods.

the various factors in the economy and the result of some autonomous technical progress. The term in brackets corresponds to the change in the sectoral structure of GDP due to changes in foreign prices or domestic taxes. It is essentially equivalent to the price index problem in the measure of GDP, and we shall ignore it in what follows, thus sticking to the standard growth accounting identity.[7]

Behavioral assumptions on the accumulation of productive factors are now necessary. A general representation of individual accumulation behavior may be given by:

$$\Delta F_{ji} = \phi\left(W_i;\ y_i;\ \frac{\pi_j}{\pi};\ \frac{w_j^a}{w^a} \right) + C_{ji} - F_{ji} \qquad (7)$$

where ΔF_{ji} is the change in factor j held by individual i. Thus Φ is the total demand for factor j by individual i and it depends on his or her wealth, W_i $(= \Sigma\ F^\circ_{ji}.\pi)$; his or her income, y_i; the expected remuneration rate of that factor, w_j^a; and its price, π_j. As only relative prices and relative returns matter, the latter two prices are deflated by some mean asset price and return. Finally, C_{ji} represents some exogenous component of factor accumulation by individual i. In the case where the individual actually refers to a 'class' of individuals, C_{ji} may correspond, for instance, to demographic growth.

Expression (7) is a general representation of a rather complex phenomenon, which requires the modelling of all asset markets. We shall not get into such detail here. What really matters here is that, directly or indirectly, the individual accumulation of factors generally appears as a nonlinear function of individual income and wealth. This implies that, in general, the aggregate accumulation of factors in the economy depends on the initial distribution of income and wealth. Aggregating expression (7) over all individuals and using previous relationships leads to the following reduced form for the growth of factor endowments:

$$\delta F_j = A_j(Y,\ W,\ p,\ t,\ F) \qquad (8)$$

where W stands for the distribution of wealth.[8]

---

[7] Note, however, that this term may be temporarily of some importance, for instance in countries undergoing trade liberalization.
[8] The way to move from (7) to (8) may be more or less complicated, depending on the phenomena to be represented and the number of factors. The link is obvious when the only

Of course, the preceding expression is valid only for the accumulable endogenous factors of production. The equivalent of expression (8) for nonaccumulable factors such as land or natural resources is an equation yielding the price of the corresponding asset. Likewise, the function A_j is a constant for factors such as labor that may be assumed to grow exogenously.

An expression similar to (8) is obtained from (6) for overall growth:

$$g = B(\Upsilon, W, p, t, F) + TP \qquad (9)$$

According to this expression, growth at a point of time is determined by the availability of productive factors, the vector of prices and market distortions, and the distribution of income and wealth at that point of time. It also depends on some exogenous technical progress or through that term effects the accumulation of productive factors not explicitly taken into account in the model.

Although extremely simple, the preceding argument helps us understand the way various mechanisms may simultaneously influence and determine growth and income distribution. Consider, for instance, a country where human capital accumulation is exogenously enhanced. The first direct consequence will be a faster rate of growth. After some time, however, the availability of human capital will affect growth endogenously through the F argument of function $B(\ )$. Other things being equal, the availability of more human capital will reduce the remuneration rate of that factor and through (7) will redirect the private accumulation process toward other factors. Both the direct change in human capital and the preceding phenomena will have some effect on the distribution of income, Υ. In turn, this will affect the overall growth rate through a change in the aggregate rate of savings in the economy.

The preceding framework is adequate to study the issues presented at the beginning of this chapter. The distribution of income (and wealth) affects growth endogenously through the accumulation of productive factors—equations (8) and (9)—and possibly exogenously through the TP factor. An empirical model seeking to determine the relationship between growth and inequality must rely on estimates of factor-accumu-

---

factor is private physical capital. It is a little less so when one includes in addition nonaccumulable assets such as land. Equation (8) is then replaced by an equation giving the price of nonaccumulable assets, that price entering in turn into the equation determining the rate of growth of accumulable factors. Adding the possibility that the vector t of tax rates may be endogenous, the growth rate in accumulable factors indeed appears as a rather complicated function of the income (and wealth) distribution.

lation equations (8); on estimates of the weight of the various factors in overall growth; and, finally, on the possible direct effect of distribution on growth through the factors hidden in *TP*. We intend to estimate a model of that type in the second part of this paper.

Steady State, Endogenous Growth, and Cross-country Comparisons

The preceding framework is adequate for studying the 'temporary' aspects of growth and the general evolution over time of any given economy. It might be inadequate, however, if one were to take a long-term or cross-sectional point of view. In the well-known Solow model[9] for instance, it is well known that the assumptions of constant saving rates and constant returns to scale lead the economy toward a steady state of growth in which the various accumulable factors grow at the same rate, n, as population, and GDP grows at the rate $n+TP$. This remains true in the presence of heterogenous individuals.[10] All individual incomes and wealth grow then at the rate TP, so that the distributions of income and wealth remain constant. With the preceding notations, the steady state of growth in a Solow model is characterized by:

$$\Delta F_j = n + TP; \qquad g = n + TP; \Delta y_i = TP$$

where j corresponds to accumulable factors and i to individuals.

It is thus clear that the distribution of income is independent from the steady state rate of growth in the Solow model. This is exogenously given by the rate of population growth and technical progress. Like behavioral parameters, the distribution of income may determine cross-country differences in the level of GDP per capita, but not its rate of growth.[11] It is only when the economy is off its steady-state path that the distribution of income may actually influence the rate of growth.

These properties are illustrated in Figure 2.1. The two economies a and b have the same rate of exogenous technical progress. Inequality is larger in economy a than b. In the steady state, the growth path of the two economies is parallel. The only difference possibly introduced by the larger inequality in economy a is that its growth path is below

---

[9] This is meant to refer to Solow's 1956 paper. However, we refer in what follows to an 'extended' Solow model in which there are various accumulable factors of production.

[10] For the treatment of income and wealth distribution in the Solow framework, see Stiglitz (1969) and Bourguignon (1981).

[11] This is the logic behind the Kuznets curve literature.

Figure 2.1. Steady Growth and Inequality in Solow Model

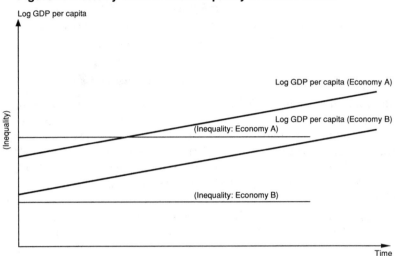

that of economy *b*, but the opposite could also be true. In Figure 2.2, it is assumed that both economies suffered the same relative shock at some point. Over time they both return to their steady growth path. It is now possible, however, that because of the difference in distribution this transition is faster in one economy than in the other.

Things would be different if one were to take the point of view of the recent endogenous growth models. Because of externalities or overall increasing returns to scale, the technical progress term of the Solow model becomes a function of the behavioral parameters of the economy. The distribution of factors among individuals may be such a parameter, although most endogenous growth models to date are cast in terms of a representative agent and do not permit us to account for inequality. The steady state of an endogenous growth model with heterogenous agents could thus be characterized by:

$$\Delta_j = mj(\dots \Upsilon, \dots)$$

$$g = \gamma(\dots \Upsilon, \dots)$$

$$\Delta y_i = \gamma(\dots \Upsilon, \dots)$$

Figure 2.2. Transition in Solow Model

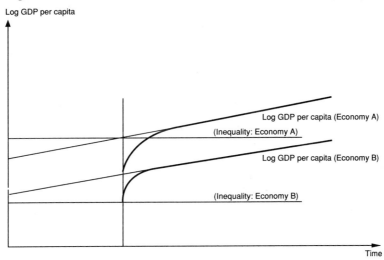

where, as before, Υ stands for the inequality of income, and the other (constant) arguments of the functions $m_j(\ )$[12], and $\gamma(\ )$ are relevant behavioral parameters of economic agents.

The relationship between inequality and growth in the case of endogenous growth is illustrated in Figure 2.3. Economy a is growing faster than economy b, and it also happens to be more egalitarian. Notice, however, that, unlike what would be observed on a transition path, there may not exist a real causality relationship here. Two cases may hold. In the first, the economies do not share the same fundamental behavioral parameters. As a consequence, both the steady growth rate and the long-term income distribution are different across both economies. There is therefore simultaneity, but no causal relationship between growth and distribution. In the second case, on the contrary, initial conditions determine the long-term equilibrium because of a mul-

---

[12] As above, the j index refers to accumulable factors. However, it may also refer to population growth, as in the endogenous growth models inspired by Becker (see, e.g., Becker, Murphy, and Tamura, 1990). This is the reason the function m is indexed by the type of factor j. The function m_j must actually be equal across all accumulable factors to be in a steady state.

Figure 2.3. Steady Growth and Inequality in Endogenous Growth Model

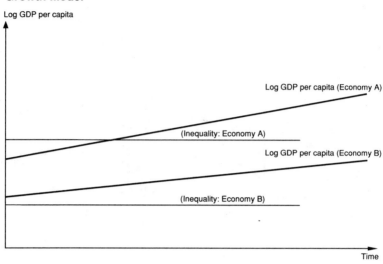

tiplicity of long-term equilibria. Economies *a* and *b* may have the same behavioral parameters, but because economy *a* was initially more egalitarian than economy *b*, it remained so and is able to grow faster. Nevertheless, the converse may also hold. A large enough change in the distribution of some factors in economy *b* might be sufficient to move it onto a growth path parallel to that of economy *a*.

The preceding distinction between steady-state and transition behavior is important to put the available cross-country evidence into proper perspective. Income distribution and growth are related either because economies are off their long-term equilibrium, or because that long-term equilibrium involves some endogenous rate of growth. However, a true causal relationship exists only if the economies are off their long-term equilibrium, or because there are multiple long-run equilibria for each of them. Note also that, from a policy point of view, a small change in the distribution of factors may have some impact on the growth of the economy on its transition path, but no influence at all on the long-term equilibrium path. In what follows we shall be working on a sample of developing countries only, and we will generally take the view that these countries are on their transition path rather than at long-term equilibrium. Indeed, the structural changes that characterize the growth process of most of these countries, especially the fastest-growing ones, suggest that they may still be far from their steady state.[13]

Growth and Distribution: Cross-country Evidence

We now investigate the empirical relationship linking growth, distribution, and the accumulation of productive factors in a cross-section of countries. As far as growth is concerned, this analysis is in the spirit of recent work by Mankiw, *et al.* (1992), itself inspired by the well-known paper by Barro (1991). As far as distribution is concerned, it is in the tradition of literature on the Kuznets curve.

The sample of countries we shall be using has been described in Bourguignon and Morrisson (1990). It is somewhat original in comparison with the cross-sections found in the literature mentioned above because it includes only small and medium-sized developing countries. Restricting the sample to developing countries permits us to avoid identifying empirical relationships only on the basis of differences between developed and developing countries, a very unsatisfactory practice. On the other hand, restricting the sample to small and medium-sized countries is equivalent to focusing on relatively open economies, an agreeable choice for the above theoretical framework. The sample includes 35 countries that have been selected based on the availability of comparable and reliable income distribution data around 1970. Its composition is given in Table 2.1 and the definition of variables is given in the note to Table 2.2.[14]

The objective of our empirical analysis is to check the validity of the theoretical framework presented in the preceding section and to test the significance of the relationship between growth, income distribution, and factor accumulation. We begin with the independent analysis of cross-country differences in per capita GDP growth, first, and then income distribution. We then consider both variables simultaneously. In all cases and in line with the objectives of this paper, we try to identify regional specificities.

Cross-country Differences in Growth

Table 2.2 shows the results of regressions on the present sample analogous to those run by Mankiw, *et al.* (1992) on a sample of approximately

---

[13] To illustrate that point, agriculture's share of GDP fell from 16 percent to less than 10 percent over the last decade in the Republic of Korea, whereas that of manufacturing rose from 28 percent to 33 percent.

[14] A more complete discussion of that sample is offered in Bourguignon and Morrisson (1990).

Table 2.2. Growth Equations[a]

	Lgdp	L(i/y)	L(n+g)	L(sec)	ppp[b]	Income dist.	Latam	Afric	R²
Tcy60	−1.89	.702	.547	1.32	−.465				.516
	(3.76)	(1.79)	(0.19)	(3.92)	(0.97)				
Tcy60	−1.26	.429	1.72	1.27	−.518		−1.72	−.566	.622
	(2.43)	(1.16)	(0.63)	(2.71)	(1.17)		(2.79)	(0.66)	
Tcy60	−1.20	.765	4.08	1.18	−.337	.197[c]			.583
	(2.10)	(2.07)	(1.27)	(3.63)	(0.74)	(2.18)			
Tcy60	−.73	.510	4.53	1.11	−.408	.165[c]	−1.56	−.600	.668
	(1.30)	(1.43)	(1.52)	(2.46)	(0.96)	(1.95)	(2.63)	(0.73)	
Tcy60	−1.40	.760	3.56	1.09	−.495	−.076[d]			.556
	(2.43)	(1.98)	(1.05)	(3.03)	(1.05)	(1.63)			

Notes:
[a] The definition of variables is as follows:

TCY:	Rate of growth of GDP per capita	Lgdp:	Logarithm of GDP per capita
GDP:	Level of GDP per capita (1985 US $)	Li/y:	Logarithm of investment rate
Prim:	Primary enrollment rate	L(n+g):	Logarithm of population growth rate +
Sec:	Secondary enrollment rate		5 per cent
Sch:	Mean years of schooling of adult population	Lsec:	Logarithm of secondary schooling enrollment
Prot:	Trade protection dummy variable	Land equal:	Share of small and medium farmers in
PPP:	Purchasing power parity		land ownership
I/Y:	Investment rate	Mines Exp:	Dummy variable for mineral exporter
Latam:	Latin America dummy variable	Agr Ex:	Dummy variable for agricultural
Afric:	Africa dummy variable		exporters

The suffix 6 or 60 indicates that the variable refers to year 1960 (for levels) or to the period 1960–85 for growth rates. T-statistics are in parentheses.
[b] Investment-based index.
[c] Inequality summarized by the share of the bottom 60 percent.
[d] Inequality summarized by the share of the top 20 percent.

100 developed and developing countries. The empirical framework used by Mankiw, *et al.* (1992) is preferred to the more general specification used by Barro (1991) and other authors in that tradition because it permitted us to stick more closely and more rigorously to the reduced-form model discussed in the preceding section.

The theoretical reference is the transition toward steady growth in the extended Solow model, in which differences in growth rates across countries are explained by the difference between equilibrium and actual GDP per capita; the larger that difference, the faster the growth. Equilibrium GDP per capita is not observed, but in theory it should depend positively on investment rates, both in physical and human capital, and negatively on the rate of population growth. Along the transition path and assuming that aggregate production is not too different across countries, national growth rates should depend positively on human and physical investment rates and negatively on the demographic growth rate and actual GDP—the so-called convergence or catching-up effect.

Under the assumption of a Cobb-Douglas production technology, the functional specification of the preceding relationship is linear with respect to the growth rate and logarithmic with respect to all the other variables—with a linear transformation for the demographic growth rate. This is the specification that has been estimated following Mankiw, et al. The explanatory variables of the GDP per capita growth rate are thus the logarithm of the share of investment expenditures in GDP (Li/y); the logarithm of the secondary school enrollment rate ($Lsec$), which has the same dimension as an investment rate; the logarithm of the level of GDP per capita ($LGDP$), expressed as comparable purchasing power parities using Heston and Summers correction coefficients; and the logarithm of the demographic growth rate (Ln).[15]

Five additional variables enter the growth equations alternatively. First is the purchasing power parity index for investment goods, which Barro (1991) argues might be a good indicator of the way market distortions may affect growth. The GDP-based purchasing power parity index measures market distortions, but also includes cross-country differences in the size of the nontradeable goods sector. It is well known that this index is strongly related to the level of GDP per capita, as prices of services and nontradeable goods tend to be lower in poor countries. Once corrected for that variable, actual market distortions may be the main source of cross-country differences in GDP-based purchasing power parity. This second variable is sometimes used in the regressions in place of the previous one. A third variable that will be considered naturally is the distribution of income. Three indicators have been used: the shares of the bottom 40 percent and 60 percent and that of the top 20

---

[15] Although it is available, the primary school enrollment rate is not used in the following regressions. Its inclusion does not modify the main conclusions obtained. Also, the correction made by Mankiw, et al. (to transform school enrollment into a true human capital investment rate defined on the whole labor force) has not been implemented here. The reason is that no attempt has been made to test all the restrictions implied by the Solow model. Finally, note that the demographic growth rate plus a constant stands for the rate of technical progress and the rate of depreciation in accordance with the Solow model. As in Mankiw, et al., that constant is arbitrarily equal to .05.

percent of the population. The last two variables are dummy variables for region. They are included to test whether cross-regional differences in growth rates are satisfactorily explained by the preceding set of variables.

The argument in the preceding section shows that many of the above explanatory variables are likely to be endogenous. This is true particularly for the investment rates in physical and human capital and for income distribution. We shall not try to correct for the resulting bias in the present exploratory set of regressions. This will be done later in this section.

The results of the most relevant regressions are reported in Table 2.3. The dependent variable is the average annual rate of growth over the period 1960–85.[16] The following features are noticeable.

First, it is interesting that the results obtained by Mankiw, et al. (1992) remain significant even when the sample is restricted to developing countries. Only one variable loses significance, namely population growth. The overall quality of the fit also compares well with the results obtained from samples including both developed and developing countries; the adjusted R^2 statistic is approximately .50 here as in Mankiw, et al. Except for population growth, all variables have the expected effect on the rate of growth. The level of GDP per capita has a negative impact, whereas the accumulation rates of both physical and human capital have a positive influence.

The introduction of the purchasing power parity index—for investment goods or the GDP-based index corrected for development differences—does not significantly improve the quality of the fit. As mentioned above, however, it is not clear whether this variable actually captures market distortions with some inhibiting effect on growth.

A second result of interest is that income equality proves to be a significant positive determinant of growth. This confirms some of the results reported by Persson and Tabellini (1991 and 1992).[17] In the present sample, this effect is rather strong since a one-percentage-point increase in the total (personal) income of the bottom 40 percent of the distribution increases the annual rate of growth by almost 0.2 percentage points. It is interesting to stress that growth seems to be more sensitive to the bottom of the income distribution than to the top,

---

[16] This is the period used in Mankiw, et al. (1992), Barro (1991), and Persson and Tabellini (1992), which should facilitate the comparison.

[17] In the present case, however, the investment rate is included as an explanatory variable, and no control is introduced for political regime as in the regressions reported by these authors. Also, our sample is restricted to developing countries, whereas theirs include both developed and developing countries.

Table 2.3. Income Distribution Equations[a]

	Const	Sec60	Prot.[b]	Land equal.	Mines exp.	Agr. exp.	Latam	Afric	n	R²
Share bottom 40%	10.66	.079	−.668	.038	−4.11	−1.35			36	.60
		(2.13)	(.91)	(2.24)	(4.29)	(1.35)				2
	10.31	.084	−2.80[b]	.041	−2.78	−1.38			19[b]	.67
		(1.46)	(2.50)	(1.57)	(1.97)	(.90)				8
	9.58	.123	−.724	.037	−4.06	−1.45	.169	1.54	36	.62
		(2.42)	(.97)	(1.88)	(4.21)	(1.35)	(.14)	(1.24)		3
Share bottom 60%	17.9	.216	−.322	.072	−5.53	−1.47			36	.66
		(3.93)	(.29)	(2.88)	(3.89)	(.93)				2
	16.5	.292	−.395	.067	−5.44	−1.64	−.186	2.46	36	.68
		(3.90)	(.36)	(2.30)	(3.83)	(1.03)	(.10)	(1.34)		7
Share top 20%	66.2	−.346	−.636	−.077	6.15	2.03			36	.61
		(4.34)	(.40)	(2.12)	(2.98)	(.88)				2
	64.3	−.258	3.79[b]	−.117	5.52	1.99			19[b]	.72
		(2.40)	(1.80)	(2.33)	(2.07)	(.69)				1
	65.5	−.434	−.679	−.049	5.96	2.14	2.82	−1.97	36	.64
		4.04	.43	1.16	2.92	.94	1.10	.75		7

Notes:
[a] See the definition of variables in Table 2.2. *T*-statistics are in parentheses.
[b] Ppp-based variable for 36–country sample, and protection dummy variable for the 19–country sample.

i.e., the share of the top 20 percent is not significant in the last regression of Table 2.2.

Finally, the role of the Latin American dummy proves to be extremely strong. Moreover, it modifies the influence on growth of both the physical investment rate and, to a lesser extent, income distribution. Other things being equal, Latin American countries tend to grow at an average annual rate approximately 1–1.5 percentage points below that in other countries in Asia or in Africa. Note that the dummy variable for the latter region is not significant. At the same time, one may notice in Table 2.3 that the introduction of the Latin American dummy variable reduces—although not significantly—the influence of the physical investment rate on growth. Of course, this is due to the fact that, on average, the rate of physical investment is lower in Latin America than in other countries (see Table 2.1). That the dummy variable for Latin America is negatively significant despite the lower rate simply means that its lower rate of physical capital accumulation over the period is not sufficient to explain its lower-than-average growth performance. The same holds to a lesser extent for the income distribution variable. Thus, the hypothesis that income inequality could be an important specific deterrent to growth in Latin America does not appear to be confirmed by this first set of results.

As stated above, however, the coefficients reported in Table 2.3 may be biased because of the endogeneity of several explanatory variables. As a first step towards the correction of a possible simultaneity bias, we now examine possible instruments to be used in explaining the income distribution variables.

Cross-country Differences in Income Distribution

Table 2.3 summarizes the results obtained in several regressions made on income distribution variables along the lines discussed in the first part of this study. Following the theoretical argument there, four sets of variables are included: factor endowments, summarized by schooling variables and the availability of natural resources (mineral and agricultural exports); the distribution of factor ownership (land and, implicitly, schooling); market distortions (protection); and regional dummy variables.[18]

The significant variables in explaining differences in income distribution across countries are secondary school enrollment, the presence of mineral resources, trade protection, and the distribution of land ownership.

The first two variables in the preceding list may correspond to factor endowments, but the secondary school enrollment rate also conveys some distributional information. School enrollment is indeed a binomial variable, the variance of which depends on its mean. It thus describes at once the amount of human capital as well as its distribution. Below an enrollment rate of 50 per cent, the variance of human capital in the population increases with enrollment, and the opposite is true for rates above 50 per cent.[19] However, as the secondary enrollment rate in almost all countries in our sample is generally below 50 per cent, it is difficult to disentangle the endowment effect from the variance effect. If both of them are present, then the results appearing in Table 2.3 show that the former dominates the latter. The variance effect should reduce the share of the bottom

---

[18] GDP per capita as a proxy for the stock of physical capital per capita was also included but did not prove to be significant.

[19] If q is the mean of a binomial variable taking the values 0 and 1, its variance is given by $q(1-q)$. That function goes through a maximum for $q=1/2$.

deciles and increase that of the top. In other words, the regression results suggest that, through its impact on factor rewards, an increase in human capital has an equalizing effect on income distribution.

The same result had already been obtained in the early work on the Kuznets curve by Ahluwalia (1976). In his sample of 60 countries, including 40 developing countries, the secondary enrollment rate as well as the literacy rate were found to be significant determinants of income distribution, along with GDP per capita and the square of that variable, in the Kuznets curve tradition. The role of education in equalizing incomes thus seems rather robust.[20]

An additional remark must be made concerning the influence of education on the distribution of income. It is that this influence depends very much on the way education enters the regression. Here, the secondary school enrollment rate in 1960 is supposed to give some indication about cross-country differences in the average individual human capital in the labor force during 1960–85.[21] Instead of using school enrollment rates (i.e., investment flows) as a proxy for the stock of human capital 15 years later, it was also possible to use direct estimates of this stock. However, replacing school enrollment rates by the mean number of years of schooling estimated by Barro and Lee (1993) led to nonsignificant results. This suggests either that there is a measurement problem in the mean years of schooling calculated by these authors or that the way education may influence the distribution of income is rather more subtle than could be expected.

The significance of the mineral export dummy variable in Table 2.3 has already been extensively discussed in Bourguignon and Morrisson (1990). It is suggested there that, although mineral exports now are publicly appropriated in most developing countries where they are substantial, this may be rather recent. The significance of that dummy variable may thus correspond to some unequalizing hysteresis effect that a highly concentrated and privately owned mineral export sector has on the income distribution. In countries where the sector initally was foreign-owned, this effect could correspond to the climate of corruption

---

[20] In Ahluwalia (1976), as in the present case, it is also reassuring to see that secondary school enrollment has a greater impact on the bottom 6 than on the bottom 4 deciles. Indeed, it is to be expected that progress in secondary education benefits the middle more than the bottom of the distribution. It must be stressed, on the other hand, that unlike in Ahluwalia (1976), GDP per capita and the literacy rate failed to be significant in this sample.

[21] It would have been possible also to include primary school enrollment, but that variable proves less or not significant when used in conjunction with secondary school enrollment. Both variables are very correlated anyway.

that this status often created. It is interesting that no such effect is present in countries specializing in primary agricultural exports once one controls for the distribution of land ownership.

Although defined on a restricted sample, the trade protection variable appears to have a very significant unequalizing influence on the distribution of income. This effect is also discussed at length in Bourguignon and Morrisson (1990) where it is suggested that it corresponds to a simple form of the Stopler-Samuelson theorem. It is remarkable that non-significant results are obtained when that variable is replaced by purchasing power parity as in the growth regressions. The status of the latter variable as an index for market distortions thus seems doubtful.

Finally, two regional dummy variables for Latin America and Africa fail to be significant, and their introduction does not modify the coefficients of the other variables in the regression. This is in marked contrast to the growth regressions and suggests that there is no strong omitted variable bias in the model that is proposed. It must be stressed in addition that this model performs rather well. An adjusted R^2 above 60 percent for a sample of developing countries only is unexpectedly high in the Kuznets curve literature.

Distribution, Factor Accumulation, and Growth

We now come to the direct estimation of the structural model presented in the first part of this chapter. Growth is the result of factor accumulation and a (possibly endogenous) technical progress term. Both this term and the accumulation of factors may be influenced by the distribution of income. On the other hand, factor accumulation rates, income distribution, and growth must be seen as mutually interdependent not only through direct causal relationships, but also because they may be jointly determined by the same set of unobserved country-specific behavioral parameters as in long-term equilibrium growth.

Possible simultaneity biases are corrected by the usual instrumental variable method. Whenever they appear on the right-hand side of an equation, the two factor accumulation rates and the income distribution variables are first regressed on a set of exogenous variables, and their fitted value is introduced in the regression. The set of instrumental variables includes the exogenous variables appearing in the growth equation (level of 1960 real GDP per capita, population growth rate, market distortions based on the purchasing power parity index) and the additional exogenous variables appearing in the preceding income distribution

Table 2.4. Factor Accumulation Equations[a]

	GDP	Sch.	ppp[b]	Dist.	Latam	Afric	R²
Sec 60	6.41	2.28	−2.06	1.61[c]			.503
	(3.85)	(2.11)	(.73)	(2.54)			
Sec 60	4.94	2.44	−3.11	−1.05[d]			.603
	(3.40)	(2.53)	(1.23)	(3.89)			
Sec 60	4.67	.964	−.854	.845[c]	−3.76	−13.4	.686
	(2.95)	(1.01)	(.36)	(1.47)	(1.04)	(3.89)	
Sec 60	3.63	1.26	−1.61	−.645[d]	.576	−10.3	.698
	(2.62)	(1.29)	(.69)	(1.80)	(.13)	(2.43)	
I/Y 60–85	.428	1.26	3.04	.208[c]			.129
	(.28)	(1.28)	(1.29)	(.36)			
I/Y 60–85	.475	1.44	−3.14	.619[d]			.141
	(.32)	(1.48)	(1.23)	(.72)			
I/Y 60–85	1.63	.956	−3.35	−.969[c]	−12.0	−6.52	.429
	(1.11)	(1.08)	(1.53)	(1.81)	(3.60)	(2.03)	
I/Y 60–85	2.71	.721	−2.59	.632[d]	−14.8	−9.33	.433
	(1.84)	(.78)	(1.18)	(1.87)	(3.65)	(2.35)	

Notes:
[a] See the definition of variables in Table 2.2. *T*-statistics in parentheses.
[b] Investment-based ppp.
[c] Share of bottom 40 percent. Instrumented variable.
[d] Share of top 60 percent. Instrumented variable.

equations (distribution of land and dummy variables for mineral and primary agricultural exports). The mean years of schooling of the working-age population as well as the regional dummy variables enter the school enrollment rate equation exogenously and are also used as instruments.

Table 2.4 shows the resulting equations for factor accumulation. Following our theoretical argument, both physical and human capital accumulation should depend on available factor endowments, market distortions, and income distribution. GDP per capita and the mean years of schooling of the labor force represent the first set of variables. Variables derived from purchasing power parity indices stand for market distortions,[22] and the shares of the bottom 40 percent and the top 20 percent represent alternatively—under the column heading 'Dist'—the

[22] As before, this variable is either the purchasing power parity on investment goods or the residual of GDP purchasing power parity over real GDP per capita.

income distribution.[23] In addition, dummy variables have been included to test for regional idiosyncrasies.

When one does not control for regions, several variables prove quite significant and powerful in explaining cross-country differences in secondary school enrollment rates. These are the level of real GDP per capita, the accumulated stock of human capital as measured by the mean number of years of schooling of the labor force, and the income distribution variable for the 1960–85 period.

The significance of the first two variables is not really surprising, although it is not clear *a priori* whether real GDP per capita corresponds to supply or demand effects in the field of education. In other words, it is difficult to tell whether more investment in education takes place because more schools have been created in the public sector or because parents want to send their children to school for a longer time. The positive influence of an egalitarian income distribution on the aggregate enrollment rate would seem to correspond more to demand effects, since it essentially means that the income elasticity of secondary school enrollment is smaller at the top of the distribution. It is also interesting that secondary school enrollment is apparently more sensitive to the top than to the bottom of the income distribution. The second regression in Table 2.4 exhibits a better fit than the first one. Indeed, in most countries it is in the middle class rather than among the poor that the income elasticity of secondary education is the highest. It is natural, then, that secondary school enrollment is better explained by the upper part of the income distribution.

The introduction of dummy regional variables somewhat modifies the preceding results. Although the fit is greatly improved, the existing stock of human capital loses statistical significance, the same being true (to a lesser extent) of income distribution, at least when it is represented by the share of the bottom 40 per cent. The explanation of these results is simply that school enrollment is lower in Africa, and that the initial positive effect of the mean level of schooling on school enrollment is partly due to the fact that this variable is also lower on average in African countries.

The preceding results are interesting because they suggest that, even when the African specificity is taken into account, secondary education may be a self-accelerating engine for growth and income equality. If one supposes that investment in human capital enhances growth, then

---

[23] The regressions run on the bottom 60 percent of the income distribution variable did not prove significantly different from those run on the bottom 40 percent.

education becomes the center of a virtuous circle for growth. Investing in human capital in an exogenous way accelerates growth; but, according to the preceding results, this increase in GDP per capita, and to a lesser extent in the mean level of schooling of the population, endogenously raises educational investments, which in turn accelerates growth. Another virtuous circle exists through income distribution. We saw in the previous sections that more investment in education meant a more egalitarian income distribution. The first regressions in Table 2.4, however, show that, other things being equal, a more equal income distribution increases school enrollments.[24] Educational investments may thus be responsible for both self-accelerating growth and self-improving income distribution.

Quite different results are obtained for the share of physical investment in GDP. Without regional dummy variables none of the explanatory variables has a significant influence on the rate of physical capital accumulation. Nevertheless, the inclusion of regional dummies drastically improves the fit of the regression and makes the role of income equality on investment negatively significant. This is the opposite of what was observed with the African dummy variable in the school enrollment rate equation. In the present case, the explanation of that phenomenon is that Asian countries are those where the rate of investment is, *ceteris paribus*, the highest and where income distribution is on average the most egalitarian. Thus the income distribution variable becomes significant only when the specificity of Asian countries has been accounted for.[25]

The other variables in the investment rate equation are not significant. Yet it may be stressed that, as could be expected, the coefficients for GDP per capita and the level of schooling are positive, and that for the ppp-based market distortion variable is negative.

That the rate of investment is positively influenced by the inequality of income distribution agrees with the intuition that if domestic savings is the ultimate determinant of investment, then the rich can be expected to save more than the poor in proportion to their relative incomes. Such a relationship, however, has seldom been put to the test. As a matter of fact, a more detailed analysis shows that, in the present case, this strong statistical relationship partly goes through the mineral

---

[24] Remember that the obvious simultaneity between the income distribution and school enrollment equations has been taken care of through the instrumentation of income distribution variables in Table 2.4.

[25] The reason we refer here to Asian specificity is that the dummy variables for Latin America and Africa in the last regressions of Table 2.4 are not statistically different.

exporter dummy variable used in the instrumentation of income distribution. It was seen in the previous section that, for reasons that are still to be identified precisely, there is more inequality in countries where exports of mineral products are important. An explanation of the observed relationship thus is that these countries, on average, invested more than others over the period under analysis. To the extent that the mineral export sector is generally controlled by the government, this is not unexpected. The positive influence of income inequality on the investment rate may thus be due to a larger public contribution to investment in mineral exporting countries. Further analysis of this point has been left for future work as it would require us to distinguish investment expenditures according to their public or private origin, something we could not do here for lack of data.[26]

The last piece of the model is the growth equation in which factor accumulation rates and income distribution have been instrumented, using all the exogenous variables of the preceding regressions. The results reported in Table 2.5 show no drastic difference in comparison with the original ones in Table 2.2. All coefficients are of a comparable order of magnitude. Some substitution has taken place between physical and human capital, however, with the coefficient of physical investment increasing and that of school enrollment decreasing in comparison with the original estimates. This would suggest that there was indeed some simultaneity bias in the original regression. The difference is, however, not really significant.

It may be seen that the coefficients associated with income distribution have a larger absolute value in the instrumented regression than in the original one. What is really important, however, is that income distribution retains a significant explanatory power, even though we might have expected its influence to disappear after correcting for simultaneity and taking explicitly into account the role of that variable in the factor accumulation rates. There may be several explanations for that result. The first is that inequality is a significant determinant in the accumulation of the implicit factors that lie behind the evolution of total productivity in human and physical capital. A second explanation is a possible misspecification of the role of income distribution in the accumulation of factors. But it is too soon to start investigating alternative specifications.

---

[26] Another useful distinction to be made would be between investment in equipment and investment in other goods, as in De Long and Summers (1991). This is again left for further work.

Table 2.5. Instrumented Growth Equations[a]

Dependent variable	Lgdp	L(i/y)[b]	L(n+g)	L(sec)[b]	ppp[c]	Income dist.[b]	R²
Tcy60	−2.15	.878	−2.13	1.39	−.319		.471
	(3.64)	(1.01)	(0.67)	(2.99)	(0.60)		
Tcy60	−1.31	1.81	.787	.933	−.067	.283[d]	.540
	(1.84)	(1.90)	(.23)	(1.87)	(0.13)	(1.98)	
Tcy60	−1.33	1.48	1.30	.707	−.358	−.163[e]	.567
	(2.08)	(1.76)	(.40)	(1.38)	(.73)	(2.40)	

Notes:
[a] See the definition of variables in Table 2.2. T-statistics in parentheses.
[b] Instrumented variables.
[c] Investment-based ppp.
[d] Share of bottom 40 percent.
[e] Share of top 20 percent.

The third explanation is that the specification of the regressions reported in Table 2.5 is incomplete because the regional dummy variables are missing. The reason is an identification problem arising from the limited number of instruments available. If for the regional dummy, variables are included in the regression, only five instrumental variables—level of schooling, distribution of land, mineral exporter dummy, agricultural exporter dummy, and demographic growth—are available to identify the role of the three endogenous explanatory variables. Only two of them were seen to be actually significant in explaining one endogenous variable or another. Thus, in the regressions reported in Table 2.5, identifiability is achieved mostly through the regional dummies. Including them as independent exogenous variables practically makes the model unidentified. Under these conditions, it is possible that the identifying assumption in the regressions reported in Table 2.5—namely that regional dummies influence growth only through factor accumulation behavior—is unsatisfactory and leaves a growth residual that appears to depend, possibly artificially, on income distribution. That residual may, in fact, depend on regional dummies, but in a more subtle way that cannot be identified with the data available in the present study.

The interpretation given to the results shown in Table 2.5 must thus be taken with extreme care. At this stage they point to various hypotheses that must be tested carefully once additional data become available that may better explain independently both factor accumulation and income distribution. Taken together, however, they confirm that growth, human and physical capital accumulation, and income distribution are indeed strongly interdependent phenomena.

Conclusion

Several lessons can be learned from the preceding results. First, the determinants of cross-country differences in growth are on the whole rather robust with respect to the composition of the sample. Results obtained in this chapter on a sample of developing countries only did not prove significantly different from those obtained with the same specification by either Mankiw, *et al.* (1992) or Persson and Tabellini (1991 and 1992). Second, income distribution characteristics appeared significant in explaining differences in the rate of accumulation of human and physical capital. A more equal distribution of income induces, other things being equal, a higher rate of secondary school enrollment and a lower rate of physical investment. Third, human resources appeared as a potentially powerful engine of endogenous growth and income equality. A better educated population means a more egalitarian income distribution, which in turn implies a higher rate of school enrollment. On the other hand, a higher GDP per capita implies more investment in education, which in turn implies faster and more egalitarian growth. Fourth, income distribution may retain some significant independent role in explaining differences in growth rates, even after its role in factor accumulation has been accounted for. Fifth, regional specificities remain extremely important in explaining not only intercountry differences in factor accumulation but possibly also overall productivity gains of labor and physical and human capital. The last two points are currently subject to some ambiguity because of a lack of relevant instruments to identify fully the model under analysis.

This lack of instruments also prevents us from giving a complete answer to the question of the relationship between Latin American idiosyncrasies in growth behavior, its performance over the 1960–85 period, and its relatively high level of income inequality. Yet some features were placed in evidence.

The Latin American specificity is most apparent in physical investment behavior, with the share of investment expenditures in GDP five percentage points below the average observed in Asian countries. This difference was shown, however, not to be the result of larger inequalities in Latin America. On the contrary, income inequality proved to have a positive influence on growth, so that the investment gap between Latin American and Asian countries is, in fact, larger than it appears. At this stage, that gap is unexplained.

No such unexplained gap was found in the accumulation of human capital, even though the larger inequality of income distribution in Latin America was shown to have a significant role in reducing secondary school enrollments. According to the figures reported in Table 2.4, the higher income inequality in Latin America might be responsible for secondary school enrollment rates being 3 percent to 4 percent below what they would be otherwise.

Finally, it is possible that some significant regional differences in growth still remain after the preceding phenomena have been taken into account. This is difficult to say at this stage because of identification problems due to a lack of satisfactory instrumental variables. Among the variables that should be introduced in the analysis, much importance should be given to trade protection and market distortions. The proxies derived from purchasing power parity indices proved to be rather unsatisfactory and largely insignificant. The dummy variable derived from effective protection for a limited subsample of countries proved to be significant in explaining differences in income distribution (see Table 2.3), but the number of countries for which it is available is too limited for it to be included in the complete model. Accounting satisfactorily for these market distortions—exogenously or endogenously—through their relationship with income distribution certainly should be seen as a priority research task if we are to obtain a better understanding of cross-country differences and Latin American specificity in economic growth mechanisms and performances.

References

Ahluwalia, M. 1976. Inequality, Poverty and Development. *Journal of Development Economics* 3(4):307–42.

Alesina, A., and D. Rodrik. 1991. Redistributive Politics and Economic Growth. Harvard University, Cambridge, Mass. Mimeo.

Anand, S., and S.M.R. Kanbur. 1985. Poverty under the Kuznets Process. *Economic Journal* 95: 42–50.

Barro, R. 1991. Economic Growth in a Cross-section of Countries. *Quarterly Journal of Economics* 106(2):407–43.

Barro, R., and J.W. Lee. 1993. International Comparisons of Educational Attainment. Harvard University, Cambridge, Mass. Mimeo.

Becker, G., K. Murphy, and R. Tamura. 1990. Human Capital, Fertility and Economic Growth. *Journal of Political Economy* 98(5):512–37.

Bourguignon, F. 1981. Pareto Superiority of Unegalitarian Equilibria in Stiglitz' Model of Wealth Distribution with Convex Saving Function. *Econometrica* 49(6):1469–75.

Bourguignon, F., and C. Morrisson. 1990. Income Distribution, Development and Foreign Trade: A Cross-sectional Analysis. *European Economic Review* 34(6):1113–32.

De Long, B., and L. Summers. 1991. Equipment Investment and Economic Growth. *Quarterly Journal of Economics* 106(2):445–502.

Mankiw, G.N., D. Romer, and D. Weil. 1992. A Contribution to the Empirics of Economic Growth. *Quarterly Journal of Economics* 107(2):407–437.

Persson, T., and G. Tabellini. 1991. Is Inequality Harmful for Growth? Theory and Evidence. Institute for International Economic Studies, Stockholm. Mimeo.

Persson, T., and G. Tabellini. 1992. Growth, Distribution and Politics. *European Economic Review* 36(2–3):593–602.

Saint-Paul, G., and T. Verdier. 1991. Education, Growth and Democracy. Delta, Paris. Mimeo.

Solow, R. 1956. A Contribution to the Theory of Economic Growth. *Quarterly Journal of Economics* 70:65–94.

Stiglitz, J. 1969. Distribution of Income and Wealth among Individuals. *Econometrica* :382–397.

The World Bank. 1990. *World Development Report 1990*. New York: Oxford University Press.

Comment

Nora Lustig

Bourguignon's chapter is a serious attempt to address the question of the role played by income distribution in explaining economic growth. In the introduction, the author states that the main hypothesis analyzed is whether economic growth in Latin America is lower than in other places because of its particularly unequal distribution of income. However, in the final analysis, the author is not really able to subject this hypothesis to full empirical testing because of the restrictions imposed by applying the econometric exercise with rigor.

The analysis of the relationship between income distribution and growth is pursued in two different ways: first, through the estimation of a modified version of the augmented Solow model presented by Mankiw, Romer, and Weil (1992); and second, by estimating the structural model outlined in the paper in which some of the exogenous variables of the Solow model (i.e., investment rates in physical and human capital and income distribution) become endogenous.

The estimation of the augmented Solow model is analogous to the exercise presented in the Mankiw, *et al.* (1992) article but applied to a subset of medium-size and small developing countries and including some additional variables such as the distribution of income. Although Bourguignon says that he had no intention of testing all the restrictions implied by the Solow model, the reader is left wishing he had. The author seems to dismiss the Solow-type model because, according to the theoretical framework described in the chapter, some of the variables in the Solow model are not exogenous. However, the performance of the Solow model is not analyzed in the light of the empirical results (for example, whether the size of the coefficients corresponds to the Solow model's prediction) and thus the discussion is left incomplete. Also, the paper does not explain what mechanism would make income distribution relevant for explaining the performance of the economy in the off-steady-state trajectory. Nor does it explain what the parameters and relationships are that would result in different trajectories in reaching the steady-state path depending on the degree of inequality.

The estimation of the modified augmented Solow model yields the conclusion that a more equal distribution of income is positively associated with growth. However, the impact is mitigated when the regression includes a dummy variable for Latin America among the explanatory variables. The high negative coefficient attached to the Latin American dummy indicates that there are other unaccounted-for factors in addition to low investment rates and high inequality, which explain the relatively worse economic performance of Latin America. As Bourguignon puts it, "the hypothesis that income inequality could be an important deterrent to growth in Latin America" is not confirmed by these results.

As mentioned above, Bourguignon is concerned that the coefficients in the modified augmented Solow model could be biased because several explanatory variables may not be exogenous. In the process of correcting the simultaneity bias, the author finds that investing in human capital has an equalizing effect on the distribution of income. This result, however, is not significant when secondary school enrollment rates are replaced by the mean number of years of schooling. The latter, as the author mentions, may indicate either that there is a problem in the way the mean years of schooling were measured or that the relationship between education and equity is more complex. One certainly would like to see this issue settled with further research. Using secondary enrollment as the education variable, the results indicate that investment in human capital may result in self-accelerating growth and self-improving income distribution. On the other hand, it was found that inequality causes the physical investment rate to be higher. Bourguignon ventures some explanation for this finding, but was not able to test it for the present paper. Thus, inequality seems to have two opposite effects on factor accumulation: positive for physical capital and negative for human capital.

The bias-growth equation corrected for endogeneity shows the same result as the one obtained by Bourguignon in the modified augmented Solow model: namely, that income distribution retains significant explanatory power over economic growth. However, the author is wary of making these results conclusive because they may be due to a misspecification of the factor accumulation equations or the impossibility of including regional dummies in this version of the model without running into identification problems. Thus, the relationship between income distribution and growth requires further empirical analysis. For the moment, according to Bourguignon, the results should be treated as tentative.

As a final comment, one should mention that Bourguignon's analysis of the relationship between income distribution and growth occurs only on the supply side (i.e., how income distribution affects the accumulation of physical and human capital). No explicit analysis is made of the link between income distribution and growth from the demand side (i.e., the nexus between income distribution, the size and composition of the domestic market, and growth). This link can arise either because of the presence of noncompetitive imports or sectorally differentiated economies of scale, externalities, or the biases and rates of technological change.

Interestingly, it has been the demand-side connection which caught the interest of Latin America's so-called structuralist economists for several decades. It would have been interesting to see some of these ideas and those of the new political economy examined in this chapter as well.

References

Mankiw, G.N., D. Romer, and D. Weil. 1992. A Contribution to the Empirics of Economic Growth. *Quarterly Journal of Economics* 107(2):407–437.

Comment

Andrés Velasco

Why is the Latin American growth performance so poor relative to that of other regions? Or, in the language of recent empirical work, why is a "Latin American dummy" often significant in cross-country regressions? That is the question that François Bourguignon tackles in this chapter. The possible explanation the paper considers is the extreme income inequality observed in Latin America—a degree of inequality worse than that of much of the rest of the developing world. Such an explanation, of course, requires establishing a firm link between income distribution and growth.

To explore this hypothesis, the author sketches a theoretical model and then performs a set of cross-country regressions, using data for developing countries alone. The empirical part is divided into two sections. In the first, Barro's (1991) results are confirmed for this particular data set—in particular, there is evidence of convergence—although the results are somewhat weaker than in the sample that includes both rich and poor nations.[1] In the second section, the author estimates an equation for distribution as a function of several instrumental variables and then uses the predicted values in a set of equations regressing factor accumulation and growth on (among other variables) income distribution.

I want to focus my comments on two issues: the theoretical reasons for presuming there is a connection between inequality and growth and the empirical evidence the chapter supplies in support of this hypothesis. On a theoretical level, the chapter presents the reduced form of an NxN

---

[1] Notice that evidence for the role of human capital is limited. This is in accordance with the results of Benhabib and Spiegel (1992).

Hecksher-Ohlin model and shows that the distribution of income will generally depend on factor endowments and government redistributive policies. It then sketches out how such a model could be made dynamic, accounting for growth as a function of a number of variables. There are two difficulties with this. First, the link between distribution and growth is not derived explicitly, though the author suggests that the mechanism at work is probably Kaldor's: people at different income levels have different savings propensities. Note, however, that this is not a feature of the standard optimizing growth model, unless restrictive utility functions are employed.[2] Second, the NxN model is complex enough in a static framework. Once factor accumulation is added, its out-of-steady-state dynamics become (at least for me) impossible to disentangle. As Mulligan and Sala-i-Martin (1993) have recently shown, the dynamics of a two-sector model are complicated enough. In addition, such systems may exhibit multiple steady states and nonunique transitional paths (Benhabib and Perli, 1993). What I propose to do, therefore, is to sketch the simplest possible model of growth and distribution and then use it to interpret the chapter's empirical results.[3]

Consider an economy in which there is a continuum of infinitely lived individuals (or households, if you prefer) indexed by i, distributed over the unit interval. Each individual holds productive capital k^i, which produces consumable output through the technology $y_i = (k^i)^\alpha$, $\alpha \leq 1$. Productive capital can be interpreted as human capital, group-specific physical capital, or an aggregate of both.[4] At each point in time an individual faces the budget constraint[5]

$$k_{t+1} = y_t - c_t = k_t^\alpha - c_t \qquad (1)$$

At time 0, each individual maximizes

$$U_0 = \sum_{t=0}^{\infty} \rho^t \log (c_t) \qquad (2)$$

---

[2] In particular, the Stone-Geary utility function delivers this result. See Rebelo (1991).

[3] I will concentrate on economic links between distribution and growth. There may be political economy links as well, as Persson and Tabellini (1991) and Alesina and Rodrik (1992) have argued.

[4] What our formulation does not allow for—at least not in the present version of the model—is for k to be interpreted as physical capital that is perfectly homogeneous across agents. In that case, borrowing and lending among groups would equalize the marginal return to productive capital.

[5] Henceforth I omit the index i, but clarity is preserved by using small case letters for individual variables and capital letters for aggregates.

subject to (1) and to the initial condition of a fixed endowment of k_0 units of capital. The Euler equation can be written as

$$\frac{c_{t+1}}{c_t} = \rho \alpha k_{t+1}^{\alpha-1} \tag{3}$$

which leads to a consumption function $c_t = (1-\rho\alpha)y_t$. Substituting this expression into (2) we have the transition equation for capital:

$$k_{t+1} = \rho\alpha \; k_t^{\alpha} \text{,} \tag{4}$$

That completes the characterization of individual behavior. Turning now to aggregation, I make the crucial assumption that $log(k_0)$ is distributed normally, with mean $m0$ and variance σ_0^2. That means that $log(k_1)$, which is just a linear function of $log(k_0)$, is also distributed normally with mean $log[\rho\alpha]+m_0$ and variance $\alpha^2\sigma_0^2$. Similarly, for $t \geq 1$, equation (4) plus our distributional assumptions yield

$$m_{t+1} = log \; [\rho\alpha] + am_t \tag{5}$$

and

$$\sigma_{t+1}^2 = \alpha^2 \; \sigma_t^2 \tag{6}$$

Define an aggregate capital stock K using a C.E.S. aggregator with parameter $\gamma > 0$:[6]

$$\log[K_t] \equiv \log\left[\int_\Omega k_t^{1/\gamma} df_t(k)\right]^\gamma = m_t + \frac{\sigma_t^2}{2\gamma} \tag{7}$$

where $f_t(k)$ is the density function associated with the distribution of k and where the second equality follows from the assumption of lognormality in the distribution. Solving (7) for m_t and substituting into (5) we obtain

$$\log[K_{t+1}] \equiv \log[\rho\alpha] + \alpha \log(K_t) - \frac{\alpha}{\gamma}[1-\alpha]\frac{\sigma_t^2}{2} \tag{8}$$

---

[6] Notice that if $\gamma=1$, the C.E.S. aggregator corresponds to the arithmetic average; if γ goes to infinity, it becomes the geometric average.

This equation, jointly with (6), determines the evolution of total assets and their variance over time. Notice that, as in the Solow model, if $\alpha < 1$, the system will converge to a steady-state K. If $\alpha = 1$, on the other hand, the system will display endogenous growth.

This scheme provides a simple account of the effect of inequality on growth. Examination of the system composed of (6) and (8) reveals several interesting points. First, the existence of inequality ($\sigma^2 > 0$) has a different effect on growth rates depending on the value of α. Inequality reduces growth in the aggregate capital stock (K_t) if $\alpha < 1$. This, of course, follows from the standard intuition that, under decreasing returns, output is maximized by spreading capital evenly across all individuals. In the constant-returns case ($\alpha = 1$), on the other hand, inequality has no effect on growth.

Notice also that inequality will decrease over time if $\alpha < 1$, for the existence of diminishing returns means that the poor accumulate capital faster than the rich. Moreover, the steady-state level of K will be independent of the initial degree of inequality. But if $\alpha = 1$, inequality is constant over time.

We are now in a position to go back to the empirics in the paper. The analysis is conducted in the style of Barro's (1991) convergence regressions, in which countries are assumed to be moving toward their corresponding steady states. In that context, one can ask how such factors as income distribution affect the speed of convergence. A first result is that ". . . other things being equal, a more equal income distribution appears to increase school enrollment." If we interpret k above as human capital—and recalling that, because of the observed tendency toward convergence, we should assume $\alpha < 1$—the result is perfectly in accord with the model. The more egalitarian the distribution, the higher the average return to human capital, and hence the higher the incentive to accumulate it further.

Notice, furthermore, that the inclusion of regional dummies does not change much in this equation. After controlling for income distribution (among other things) the peculiarity of Latin America disappears, at least with regard to the process that determines the speed of human capital accumulation.

In the equation for physical capital, on the other hand, ". . . the rate of investment appears to be positively influenced by the inequality of income distribution." This result is less readily reconciled with the model above. If k is interpreted as physical capital, then borrowing and lending across individuals would ensure that they all face the same interest rate, and therefore investment behavior should depend only on the aggregate K, not on its distribution. If, on the other hand, k embodies both human and physical capital, so that its rate of return cannot be equalized across agents, the result that inequality increases investment can be obtained—but only under the assumption that there are increasing returns ($\alpha > l$). Recall, nonetheless, that the evidence for convergence in the growth regressions seems to suggest a world in which $\alpha < l$.

The author interprets the finding that inequality accelerates investment in physical capital as evidence in favor of what I have called the Kaldor hypothesis—that the rich save and invest more than the poor and that therefore growth is swifter when wealth is concentrated. Is this link present in the above model? Yes, but under two conditions: first, that k should be interpreted as an aggregate of human and physical capital, so that the marginal products of capital held by each household are not equalized; and second, that there exist increasing returns to scale ($\alpha > l$)—in that case, the more capital you have, the higher the marginal return, and therefore the higher the desired investment and savings.

Finally, the paper presents regressions in which growth is explained by (instrumented) factor accumulation and distribution variables. The results of previous equations hold up—in particular, income distribution remains significant. This also makes sense in terms of the above model, in which income distribution is only a function of initial conditions and of time, not of growth or the level of income. Therefore, correcting any perceived simultaneity bias by instrumenting should not change things much.

In short, the empirical estimates suggest that there may indeed be a role for inequality in explaining factor accumulation and growth. These links, this comment has argued, can also be rationalized in terms of a very simple model. The evidence is suggestive, but, as the author himself stresses, the scarcity of data and the complexity of the relationships studied require that conclusions be regarded only as tentative. Other empirical results linking growth and distribution—in particular those trying to capture a political mechanism, as in Persson and Tabellini (1991) and Alesina and Rodrik (1991)—are not altogether robust, as Perotti (1992) has suggested. As far as the "difference" in Latin American growth performance is concerned, inequality may have some explanatory power, but we may also have to look beyond it to get a full explanation of this puzzling phenomenon.

References

Alesina, A., and D. Rodrik. 1991. Distribution, Political Conflict and Economic Growth: A Simple Theory and Some Empirical Evidence. In *Political Economy, Growth and Business Cycles*, eds. A. Cukierman, Z. Hercowitz, and L. Leiderman. Cambridge, Mass.: The MIT Press.

Barro, R. 1991. Economic Growth in a Cross-section of Countries. *Quarterly Journal of Economics* 106(2): 407–43.

Benhabib, J., and R. Perli. 1993. Uniqueness and Indeterminacy: Transitional Dynamics in a Model of Endogenous Growth. Research Report 93–13, C.V. Starr Center for Applied Economics, New York University.

Benhabib, J., and M. Spiegel. 1992. The Role of Human Capital and Political Instability in Economic Development. Research Report 92–24, C.V. Starr Center for Applied Economics, New York University.

Mulligan, C., and X. Sala-i-Martin. 1993. Transitional Dynamics in Two-Sector Growth Models. *Quarterly Journal of Economics* 108 (August): 739–73.

Perotti, R. 1992. Fiscal Policy, Income Distribution and Growth. Discussion paper 636 (November), Columbia University.

Persson, T., and G. Tabellini. 1991. Growth, Distribution and Politics. In *Political Economy, Growth and Business Cycles*. See Alesina and Rodrik, 1991.

Rebelo, S. 1991. Growth in Open Economies. Policy Research Working Paper No. 799. Washington, D.C.: The World Bank.

3

Decentralization and Development: The Chilean Experience

Mario Marcel[1]

Decentralization is one subject on which even the most diverse political and social actors in Latin America seem to agree. They see decentralization as a solution to the long history of government incompetence, lack of participation, and geopolitical, social, and ecological imbalances.

Economists have their own arguments about decentralization, which they view as a determinant of the state's economic efficiency. In particular, they point out that the shift of responsibilities and fiscal authority to subnational levels of government may result in a balance between action by the state and the preferences of the citizenry, thus maximizing social well-being.

From both the theoretical and the practical point of view, a strong correlation seems to exist between decentralization and development. International comparisons have shown that while in the industrialized countries spending at the subnational level accounts for around one-third of total public spending, this proportion shrinks to around 15 percent in the developing countries.[2] It is further stated that the principal recent reforms pertaining to decentralization have been concentrated in the developed countries.

[1] The author wishes to thank José Espinoza and Jaime Crispi for their valuable collaboration and Sylvia Maxfield, Eduardo Modiano, Gustav Ranis, Mario Rotschild, and David Vetter for their comments.
[2] Bahl and Linn (1992), p. 392.

In spite of these trends, the demand for decentralization is clearly great and evolving rapidly. While the periods of greatest growth have required the expansion and improvement of infrastructure at all levels, economic crises have generated pressures for more intensive social action aimed at people's specific needs. Urbanization and the growth of large cities have created new and increasing demands in the areas of transport, environmental protection, and community services. It seems impossible for a highly centralized state to respond efficiently to these needs.

For these same reasons, the slowness and vacillating course of decentralization in practice are giving rise to constant disappointment and skepticism in the region. These problems are often attributed to policymakers, who approach the process in a very conservative fashion. Nevertheless, the experience of Latin America and the rest of the developing world demonstrates that the complexities of the decentralization process reach much farther and encompass political, administrative, and fiscal issues. For the central government of a developing country, decentralization generally means shifting resources, responsibilities, and power to entities whose experience and competence raise serious questions and promise uncertain results. Under such circumstances, the cautious attitude of many authorities in considering the bolder reform proposals is not surprising.

The Chilean experience, which focuses on the municipalities, is frequently cited not only as successful, but as a paradigm worthy of imitation by other developing countries. During the eighties, a bold process of transferring resources and responsibilities to municipalities was carried out in Chile, and highly innovative mechanisms were devised for financing local investment and for providing and operating social services. The nineties have seen the strengthening of municipal autonomy, the democratization of its administration, and the creation of a regional level of government, a process carried out in a framework of economic growth and democratization. Decentralization in Chile has thus not only advanced swiftly but has gone hand in hand with the country's economic and political development of the past decade.

Much of this progress stems from the fact that the convergence of interests in connection with decentralization has been especially marked in Chile. In one of the hemisphere's most centralized countries, with a monolithic state and practically no tradition of subnational governance, decentralization was, in the last decade, successfully turned into an essential component of a whole array of political projects. For the politically authoritarian and economically liberal regime it furnished the opportunity to construct a network of operative agents of the central government and a sophisticated system of participation without democracy in local administration.[3] In center-left quarters, the municipalities and local government were seen as a means of bringing state action and civil society together.[4]

The Chilean case is thus of special interest for purposes of exploring the link between decentralization, democratization, and development. Its study makes it possible to analyze a constantly changing experience and to gain important insights applicable to other countries from its successes and problems.

This paper is intended to contribute to those studies by integrating the economic, fiscal, administrative, and political aspects of the Chilean experience and focusing on the case of the municipalities. To that end, the next section examines the economic foundations of decentralization and the conditions required for decentralization actually to raise the efficiency of public administration. Those conditions are subsequently compared with the local government model that began to take shape in Chile during the eighties. The validity of that model and the problems and advantages of the current system prevailing in Chile are assessed, and changes required for the future are discussed. The paper concludes with a review of the insights on decentralization and development gained from the Chilean experience.

Criteria and Mechanisms for Decentralization

Over the years, decentralization at the local level has occupied an important place in the economic literature on fiscal federalism. Most of the studies have used macroeconomic analysis instruments to relate resource allocation at the community level to community well-being and to the state's objectives. The best-known approaches in this respect are those of community-level decisions and those of principal agent. The former seeks to establish the conditions under which decentralization maximizes economic efficiency, while the latter attempts to determine the optimum incentives that will induce local governments to meet the objectives delegated by the central government.[5] These approaches have generally centered on the developed countries, to which most of the empirical work on this topic refers.

---

[3] See Tomic and González (1983).
[4] In this connection, see the works contained in Borja, et al. (1987) and in Raczynski and Serrano (1992).
[5] For an examination of these approaches, see Campbell (1991).

Economic Foundations of Decentralization

A direct result of the economic analysis in this field has been to derive a set of economic foundations for decentralization. These can be summarized in four postulates:[6]

•   The provision of goods and services by the subnational governments permits the adjustment of that provision to the needs and preferences of the community, when these needs and preferences tend to differ among the various sectors.

•   Moreover, when the actions of subnational government are funded by local taxes and fees, the rationality of collective decisions is maximized since the community is affected by the economic cost of those decisions.

•   The exercise of public functions at the subnational level permits the introduction of competition and market factors into public administration, thereby promoting efficiency in resource allocation.[7]

•   The existence of subnational entities with fiscal authority permits increased mobilization of public resources by improving the capacity to tax the most developed activities, encouraging compliance with tax laws, and applying means of charging for the use of public services.[8]

From an economic point of view, then, decentralization is justified by diversity. Where public goods and services exist that are consumed in a differentiated spatial pattern, by communities with diverse preferences, subnational governments can increase the general welfare by adjusting the collection and allocation of public resources to the priorities and capacity of their communities. For the same reasons, a system of decentralization is efficient when subnational governments are able to take advantage of local resource allocation and have the fiscal authority to do so. In the following section we shall look at the most characteristic fiscal functions and attributions in this respect, applied to the specific case of local governments.

Functions

Musgrave (1959) and other authors have maintained that a solid basis exists for keeping responsibilities over the governmental functions of

---

[6] See Bird (1990), Shah (1991), and Bahl and Linn (1992).

[7] Such competition can be of four different kinds: (1) political competition through the electoral process; (2) competition to attract users of social services, in which there is free movement of such users; (3) territorial competition, in which there is geographic movement of inhabitants; and (4) competition for public resources.

[8] Bahl and Linn (1992), p. 386.

macroeconomic redistribution and stabilization centralized. It is also possible to argue that the higher levels of government should provide certain public goods of a national character (justice, defense, internal order, external relations), exercise regulatory functions over private activities of similar scope (regulation of the financial marketplace and natural monopolies), and build the necessary infrastructure for the nation's productive development (highways, ports, irrigation systems).[9]

The comparative advantages of local governments, in turn, reside in the provision of goods and services whose benefits are perceived at the local level and that can be delivered in different ways consistent with the community's preferences. Thus, to paraphrase Oates's "decentralization theorem," each public service should be provided by the jurisdiction that has control over the smallest geographic area to which the benefits and costs of such provision pertain.[10] Some authors also maintain that reasons of productive efficiency would justify the local provision of goods and services in some cases where economies of scale or greater administrative capacity exist at lower levels of the state.[11]

Thus, the functions economically most appropriate to the municipalities include regulation of the use and development of communal infrastructure, most notably transport and urban land use; provision of public services such as garbage collection; protection of the citizens' safety; and provision and maintenance of community infrastructure (parks, community and sports centers). These actually constitute the most traditional fields of municipal action.

Together with the foregoing, the existence at the municipal level of advantages regarding resource allocation and the production of goods and services calls to mind other areas in which centralized management presents inherent diseconomies of scale, rigidities, and administrative inefficiency. One example would be social services requiring careful targeting and specificity (social assistance) or the administration of a large number of small units, such as schools or health centers. In such cases, where the presence of substantial externalities requires the enforcement of minimum standards for quantity and quality of service, procedures can be devised to share responsibility between the central and local levels.[12]

---

[9] We use the term "higher levels of government" insofar as some of these functions can be performed by the national government or state governments, depending on the centralized or federal nature of a given country.

[10] Oates (1972).

[11] For some examples of economies of scale at the local level, see Bahl and Linn (1992), pp. 414–15.

[12] For cases of productive efficiency and administrative simplification in the municipalities, see Campbell (1991), pp. 22–25.

Funding

The municipalities have four possible sources of revenue: taxes, fees for services, borrowing, and transfers.

With respect to taxes, the central government has clear advantages from the standpoint of equity and efficiency in applying progressive taxes on income (of businesses and individuals), which lend themselves to macroeconomic stabilization (indirect taxes on domestic transactions and external trade) and which are applied on unequally distributed bases or on mobile factors of production (taxes on labor).

Local governments can more efficiently tax less mobile factors, which allows such taxes therefore to be applied at geographically differentiated rates. Municipal administration of taxes on the use of infrastructure and on activities with externalities at the local level is also appropriate. The property tax is the most characteristic of the former, and the automobile tax, of the latter.[13]

Application of fee-for-service systems is not only desirable from the administrative point of view for services performed at the local level; it is especially advisable for reasons of efficiency in that it allows the consumer a more direct and viable choice.[14] Moreover, there do not appear to be any theoretical objections to municipalities borrowing under conditions similar to those of the central government to finance their activities, but the practical objections in this case are particularly strong for the authorities charged with maintaining fiscal discipline.[15]

As a final consideration, the most powerful economic rationale for transfers from the central level to the municipalities relates to the financing of functions involving significant externalities that are not completely covered at the local level. In these cases, the existence of transfers equivalent to benefits not appropriated at that level would prompt the municipalities to provide the corresponding goods and services at a scale consistent with the maximization of social well-being, without altering the allocation of municipal resources beyond what local preferences determine.

Alternatively, transfers can also serve as a mechanism to ensure fiscal equity among different municipalities when the tax base and the demands on them are unequally distributed. In that case the most satisfactory mechanism would be to transfer to each municipality an amount equivalent to the difference between its revenues and expenditures and

---

[13] A complete theoretical and empirical examination of local taxation and its economic effects is found in Bahl and Linn (1992), part II.

[14] Bahl and Linn (1992), part III; World Bank (1988).

[15] Bahl and Linn (1992), part III; World Bank (1988).

the average or a minimum service standard.[16] Since figures for a substantial number of municipalities would exceed those benchmarks, one way of operating a compensatory transfer system would be through a fund for the redistribution of resources, without contributions from the government.[17]

Optimal Budgetary Structure

Economic efficiency in municipal government requires a specific relationship between sources of municipal funding and the expenditures necessary to perform its functions. The World Bank has summarized these relationships under four main points:

- The cost of providing local services ought to be recovered, to the extent possible, by charging the users. Such charges should reflect individual consumption or, if that is not possible, a measure of the individual benefit received.
- Services whose costs cannot be recovered by charges can be funded through general taxes—property tax, business taxes, and consumption taxes—assessed within the respective jurisdictions.
- If the benefits of the local services are extended to other jurisdictions or produce a national benefit, transfers from higher levels of government should finance such services in proportion to their external benefits.
- Borrowing is an appropriate way of financing at least some local investments, provided they do not affect the macroeconomic fiscal equilibrium.[18]

---

[16] To this end, Shah (1991) has postulated a system of compensatory transfers that would ensure fiscal equity without weakening the incentives to tax control at the local level. Under this system, such transfers would amount to the sum of: (1) the difference between the revenue generated by a representative tax system in the respective municipality and the average, and (2) the difference between the standardized expenditure per inhabitant of that municipality and the national average for standardized municipal expenditures per inhabitant (pp. 41–46).

[17] There are many systems of transfers from the central government to the municipalities. These can be defined on the basis of three characteristics: the existence of limits to the volume of the transfers, the existence of conditionality, and the requirement of cofinancing set by the municipalities. It can generally be stated that conditionality and the imposition of limits to the volume of transfers represent suboptimal solutions in cases where problems exist with respect to incentives and control from the central government to the municipalities. For a complete analysis of alternative transfer systems, see Shah (1991), pp. 22–29, and Bahl and Linn (1992), chapter 13.

[18] World Bank (1988), p. 159.

Table 3.1. Local Governments: Optimal Budgetary Structure

Functions	Financing
General administration	Property taxes
Urban regulation	Vehicle taxes
Provision of local public goods	Taxes and duties on local activities
Provision of local public services	User fees
Investment in infrastructure	Debt Taxes on improvements (when the benefits favor a specific group or sector) Capital transfers (when externalities exist)
Provision of services with externalities	Current transfers with cofinancing
Provision of services with economies of scale at the local level, large externalities, and minimal levels of provision	Open transfers without cofinancing

Based on these considerations, an "optimal budgetary structure" can be defined at the municipal level, including the most appropriate functions and funding sources and the most efficient relationship between them. This structure is presented in Table 3.1.

Following the classification of Table 3.1, the general costs of municipal administration, regulation, and provision of public goods whose apportionment among members of the community cannot be directly measured or indirectly assessed should be financed through local taxes. The most appropriate for this purpose are real estate taxes, vehicle taxes, and other taxes and fees on local activities. To the extent that the municipalities have the fiscal authority to determine their outlays and revenues, the local community could choose the combination of services it wants through the political process, paying their economic cost.

On the other hand, charging the users is the most efficient financing mechanism for public services at the local level. The charges can be supplemented by transfers from the central level when the services generate externalities outside the communal sphere.[19] In the extreme case in

---

[19] A particular mechanism that combines elements of a real estate tax and a charge for services is the so-called tax on improvements, which is levied on the greater value of the properties benefiting from local public investment projects. This tax can take the form of a special tax or be levied as part of a system to reappraise property taxes.

which such externalities prove significant and the municipal administration finds its rationale more in considerations of productive efficiency, these transfers can expand until they include the total cost of providing the services in question.

Under optimum conditions, borrowing would be an appropriate mechanism for financing investments, for under optimum conditions the municipalities would enjoy incentives to maximize the social cost-effectiveness of their projects, and payment flows would match investment returns. Where investment returns benefit only specific sectors of the population, taxes on improvements not only ensure the ability to service the debt but also expand choice at the local level, thus increasing efficiency. In contrast, where investment returns extend beyond communal boundaries, a capital transfer system is required to adjust the externalities. Nevertheless, in those cases in which borrowing is limited by fiscal considerations, these transfers should be expanded to encompass the portion of the municipal investment that is externally restricted.

Efficiency and Decentralization

The effects of decentralization on economic efficiency depend on two basic assumptions:

- the existence of fiscal flexibility at the local level, expressed in the municipal authorities' autonomous ability to match their revenues and expenditures to community preferences; and
- the existence of individual and collective decision mechanisms on the part of the public, expressed either in the geographic mobility of community residents or in democratic mechanisms of decision and control over municipal activity.

While the latter condition makes it possible to reveal the community's preferences, the former holds the key to realizing those preferences.

The foregoing conditions do not come about easily. Fiscal flexibility is rarely comprehensive enough, and it is often limited by the fiscal authorities or by institutional factors intrinsic to national public administration.[20] In these cases the quest for greater efficiency is often limited to ensuring certain minimum "levels" of municipal financial autonomy.

---

[20] Bird (1990) notes that local governments are often actively dissuaded from trying to make adequate use of local fiscal resources through a broad range of central authorizations, controls, and obstacles to anything from short-term borrowing to stabilize cash flows to the application of rates on public services and local taxes (p. 283).

Geographic mobility, moreover, cannot always be assumed to exist in developing countries, so the possibility of local choice depends primarily on the presence of institutional decision-making mechanisms. Of such mechanisms, three stand out: (1) democratic designation of municipal authorities with the proper mandate for realizing the citizens' preferences; (2) electoral or paraelectoral means for citizens to express their preferences; and (3) monitoring, inspection, and control systems available to the municipal authorities.

It should also be pointed out that the foregoing mechanisms can hardly be taken for granted in the developing world. In many countries the local authorities are appointed by the central government. In others, elected authorities have terms of office that are too short to be able to identify and act on the community's priorities. The machinery for local governance is often less developed than that for national governance.[21]

The fact that in these circumstances the contribution of municipalities to efficiency in public administration is questionable leaves open two alternative avenues. The first is to seek suboptimal solutions for shifting functions and resources to the municipalities that retain some elements of efficiency. These include centralized control of administration and municipal financing, the establishment of transfer funds, centralized project evaluation, substitution of credits granted by the central government for external credits, calling for bids to allocate transfers, and contributions from the central government. The second is to reduce the degree of autonomy of local decisions by transforming the municipalities into agents of the central government charged with meeting the objectives delegated by the latter.[22] Practically all the concrete experiences of decentralization combine elements of decentralization and delegation present in these two models.

---

[21] Campbell (1991), pp. 16–17. To these problems must be added the difficulties typical of social choice systems intended to generate coherent sets of preferences through the electoral process, expressed in the so-called Arrow's impossibility theorem (Arrow, 1950).

[22] In this case, the type of problem that arises corresponds to what is defined in the literature as relations between agent and principal. Here the efficiency of the system depends on its ability to develop sufficient incentives to ensure that the agent (municipality) accomplishes the principal's objectives at the least cost. Campbell (1991) argues that these approaches are the most effective for the advanced design of policies designed to alleviate poverty and protect the environment (p. 8).

Decentralization in Chile: The Case of the Municipalities

Municipal Reforms

Until the mid-seventies the municipalities had a minor role as centers of government in Chile. With the exception of short-lived federalist episodes such as that of the "autonomous commune" at the end of the last century, municipalities were limited to urban regulation and to cleaning and sprucing up their local areas. Municipalities had little administrative and financial autonomy to carry out those functions; their revenues were heavily dependent on the central government and their budgets were part of the national budget. Municipal personnel were poorly qualified and composed mainly of administrative functionaries (as in the rest of the civil service), and municipal government was heavily politicized.[23]

The marked dependence of the municipalities on the central government was accentuated during the first few years of military government, when numerous intervention mechanisms were established, including direct appointment of mayors by the president.[24]

This situation changed radically from the late seventies through much of the following decade. During that period, far-reaching reforms substantially expanded the municipalities' responsibilities and resources. This process can be divided into two stages: the reforms launched by the military regime from 1976 to 1989, and the municipal and regional reforms initiated with a constitutional reform in 1991 and extending into the present.

The principal changes introduced by the reforms carried out under the military regime are provided below.[25]

• Responsibilities: Municipal responsibilities were specified and substantially expanded. While conventional functions were institutionalized in urban areas, social functions were greatly expanded; municipalities began to share responsibilities with the central government in educa-

---

[23] Background information on Chilean municipalities before the reforms can be found in Tomic and González (1983) and Bravo (1992).

[24] This situation continued until 1988, when the procedure laid down in the Constitution of 1980 went into effect. Under this procedure, mayors were to be appointed on the basis of nominations put forward by local corporative bodies, the Communal Development Councils (CODECOs).

[25] For an in-depth analysis of municipal reforms in the context of changes in the organization and role of the state, see Tomic and González (1983).

tion, health, culture, recreation, sports, job creation, housing, and social assistance.[26]

• Financing: A special financing system was established, supported by taxes levied exclusively for municipal purposes. These consisted of property (real estate) taxes, vehicle taxes (driver's licenses), and taxes on productive and business activities. To this was added a system to redistribute these resources, the Municipal Common Fund, designed to compensate municipalities of communes with smaller tax bases. In addition, charges were established for some municipal services, such as garbage collection.[27]

• Administration: The administrative and financial autonomy of the municipalities was expanded, primarily by allowing them to manage their own budgets. However, budgeting had to follow the same rules on financial administration that governed other public agencies.[28]

• Rationalization: The internal organization of municipalities was restructured, including the creation of technical planning units and social departments. Staffing patterns were changed at the same time, to bring in professionals and technicians.[29] Subcontracting to the private sector was permitted for some services and financial rationalization measures were taken, such as making municipalities pay for street lighting.

• Transfers: Systems for funding investments and projects of local interest were created at the central government level. The most important of these systems is the National Fund for Regional Development (FNDR). This fund, set up in 1975, finances investments in productive and social infrastructure at the local level through a decentralized project identification and selection process in which annual resources are allocated to the regions based on a formula and distributed within the regions by the Regional Development Councils (CODEREs).[30]

• Shifting of social services: Responsibility for the administration of public institutions of learning and primary health centers was shifted to the municipalities. Transfer systems were established at the

---

[26] Organic Constitutional Law on Municipalities of 1985. Its provisions are summarized and commented upon in Ministry of the Interior (1992).

[27] Municipal Revenue Law of 1979. This legislation also established the system for shifting functions to the municipalities.

[28] See Castañeda (1990), pp. 293–294, for an analysis of changes in municipal budget procedures.

[29] The new organizational structure is contained in the Organic Constitutional Law on Municipalities. Municipal personnel administration is currently governed by the Municipal Employees Statute of 1989, which is almost identical to the Administrative Statute governing work rules and compensation in the central administration.

[30] Castañeda (1990), p. 291.

central government level. The systems operate on the basis of the benefits granted by these establishments.[31] The work rules for the personnel involved, which are governed by the norms covering private contracts with respect to compensation and dismissal, were also liberalized. In addition, the municipalities were made responsible for providing financial assistance to families in extreme need.

These reforms were applied throughout the 1980s and required considerable efforts to be put into practice and consolidated. During that time the reforms encountered serious economic, administrative, and political obstacles, and it became evident that some were insurmountable because they were rooted in basic features of the military regime's approach to decentralization.

In the first place, the expansion of municipal responsibilities and resources had to be carried out through a local administration of limited capacity. Despite the assignment of professionals to the municipalities, it is obvious that in most cases the technical and administrative capacity of those municipalities was inferior to that of the central government agencies whence the professionals came. This situation was aggravated by the imposition of new responsibilities without thorough consultation at the central level, as in the case of the removal of families in extreme need to certain specific communes or of the implementation of emergency job programs, and it has been especially serious in smaller and poorer communes.

These difficulties notwithstanding, the programs of transfers from the central government continued to grow. To the expansion of the FNDR, through a loan from the Inter-American Development Bank in 1985, were added programs to build health stations and programs to encourage local labor-intensive investment, the sum of these programs equalling the municipal component of the FNDR.[32] In this way the external funding sources for municipal investments grew steadily, until they surpassed the availability of local resources for investment.[33]

---

[31] The educational subsidy system is governed by its own legal rules, in effect since 1980. Municipal health, on the other hand, operates on the basis of voluntary agreements between the municipalities and the Ministry of Health.

[32] Not all FNDR investments can be considered to be of local benefit. While infrastructure investments in education, health, community services, and street lighting clearly relate to municipal functions, road construction and improvement has a wider scope.

[33] According to the World Bank (1992), toward the end of the 1980s only half the budgeted investment was being funded with the municipalities' operational surplus. Furthermore, the investments made through the National Fund for Regional Development, which are not recorded in the municipal accounts, must also be considered.

The central government's policies were also putting their stamp on the municipalities' social efforts. The expansion of the financial assistance programs to families in extreme need, the major emergencies during the crisis of 1982–83, and the development of specifically targeted programs such as the CAS card set the municipalities on an essentially assistance-oriented course. By the end of the eighties this course was evident not only in programs implemented jointly with the central government but also in social programs devised by the municipalities themselves.[34]

For education and primary health, the transfer process became so complex during the first half of the eighties that it had to slow the pace originally set for it. The main problems were economic in origin. The funding system was initially designed to cover the operating costs of the establishments transferred to the municipalities on the basis of standard costs per attending student (education) or per benefit (health). During the 1982–83 crisis, however, the government stopped indexing these subsidies, which shrank in real terms throughout almost the whole decade. The municipalities responded by cutting the pay of transferred personnel. In the case of education, the economic problem worsened with the transfer of students to the fledgling sector of subsidized private education, and teachers were laid off in large numbers. Toward the end of the period these factors, coupled with the sense of deteriorating quality of transferred services in the community, had led to profound questioning of the municipal decentralization system, and its future was uncertain.[35]

Finally, as municipal reforms were applied in the eighties, the weight of the system's authoritarianism and central control became especially evident. Mayors were invested with broad powers, and during a significant part of the period reported directly to the president. Although that made it possible to impose a high degree of financial discipline, the operation of the municipalities came to depend almost exclusively on the mayor's preferences and interests and the central government's policies, leaving little room for local initiative. Arbitrariness flourished in the internal administration of the municipalities and the transferred services, especially with respect to personnel. Although municipal reforms were justified in part by the municipalities' previous politicization, toward the end of the military government the munici-

---

[34] See Raczynski and Serrano (1988).
[35] The administrative problems stemming from the decentralization of these sectors should not be underestimated either. The previously mentioned limited technical capacity of the municipalities combined with major regulatory problems forced successive modifications of the subsidy systems. The most recent of those modifications took place in 1992.

palities were performing direct control and propaganda tasks. In this way, the initial project of an upgraded local administration and of a system of participation without democracy, in which municipal decisions were made with corporate support, was consciously absorbed by authoritarianism pure and simple.

The new government that took office in March 1990 faced tough challenges. While decentralization was quickly recognized as a political priority, the municipal model inherited from the military regime had to be modified. This touched off a new reform process in 1991 that is still underway at this time. The changes adopted in this period encompass political, economic, and administrative aspects of decentralization.

• Institutional changes: A constitutional reform approved at the beginning of 1992 democratized municipal administration by providing for the election of mayors and council members. The latter sit on a communal council responsible for approving the communes' plans and projects and monitoring the mayor's actions.[36] Municipal autonomy is enshrined in the Constitution. Regional governments were created, as legal entities with their own capital and competence especially concentrated in the field of investment. The regional governments are administered through a mixed formula in which an intendant (appointed by the president and a collegiate body) and the regional council (elected through an indirect system) share executive authority.[37]

• Investments: The regional governments' responsibility in the allocation of resources for public investment in new areas has been expanded. This was done by establishing a mechanism for the regional allocation of sectoral investment (ISAR), through which investment funds authorized in sectoral ministry budgets are distributed by the regional councils among specific projects in each region.[38]

• Financing: Changes to the municipal revenues system were proposed in order to augment municipal receipts and to allow greater

---

[36] For a description of the powers of the mayor and the communal council, see Ministry of the Interior (1992).

[37] Ministry of the Interior (1992), chapter II, spells out the responsibilities of the regional authorities.

[38] The following are currently proceeding under the ISAR system: investments in community equipment and urban roads of the Ministry of Housing, the secondary roads program of the Ministry of Public Works, the neighborhood and urban improvement programs of the Ministry of the Interior, the sports investment programs and a significant part of the programs of the Solidarity and Social Investment Fund. Resources involved in these programs amount to $120 million, which represents 9 percent of public investment in 1993.

flexibility in real estate tax administration and in charges for services rendered to users.[39]

• Administration: Personnel administration was improved by increasing compensation to municipal employees and encouraging older staff to retire. A restructuring of staffing patterns was proposed by increasing the numbers of professionals and technicians, introducing true career ladders, and permitting the use of temporary contract workers.[40]

• Education and health: The decentralization of education and health services was strengthened by correcting distortions in the subsidy systems and resolving the labor and compensation problems that formed the chief source of resistance to their administration on the part of the municipalities.[41]

It is evident, therefore, that the decentralization process in Chile has followed two parallel tracks. On the one hand, institutional and legal reforms have been broad, bold, and deep, reaching up to the constitutional level. In a short time these reforms have covered all aspects of decentralization, so it is not surprising that they are cited as a paradigm worthy of imitation by other countries. On the other hand, the country has traveled the more tortuous road of practical decentralization. In this less well-known and infrequently discussed area, implementation problems have been numerous, and the various aspects of the reform have sometimes clashed.

Before going on to a more detailed analysis of the theoretical and practical problems of the decentralization process in Chile, we will devote the rest of this section to an overview of the municipal model that emerges from this experience. This requires an examination of its financial aspects as well as its economic efficiency by the standards outlined in the preceding section.

Funding

Trends in municipal finance in recent years have been dominated by three factors: (1) enactment of the Municipal Revenues Law; (2) creation of subsidies for the financing of health- and education-related tasks shifted to the municipalities; and (3) increase in other transfers from the central government.

---

[39] These reforms are currently under discussion in the National Congress.

[40] Many of these changes took effect in 1992. Municipal staffing changes still await legislative approval.

[41] The reforms of the labor system and to primary health financing are contained in the draft Statute on Municipal Primary Health Care, currently under discussion in Congress.

The increase in the municipalities' own revenues has been the most significant and durable of those factors. As is shown in Figure 3.1, additional revenues generated by the Municipal Revenues Law made it possible to double the municipalities' own revenues, despite the fact that direct fiscal contributions had simultaneously been abolished. Since this reform, in addition to increasing the tax burden, meant redirecting tax revenue to the municipalities, the increase in municipal revenues was partly offset by a reduction in fiscally destined tax revenues.

Nevertheless, after strong initial growth the municipalities' own revenues stopped rising during a good part of the eighties as a result of the economic crisis early in the decade. In fact, in the recession of 1982–83 municipal revenues dropped by more than 20 percent in real terms, to recover slightly in the following years.[42]

Meanwhile, transfers for the funding of shifted services allowed a further doubling of municipal revenues; by the end of the eighties they accounted for 40 percent of total current municipal revenues. However, spending rose at about the same pace, and the transfers had to be accounted for and administered separately from other municipal funds. Soon after the new system got underway, the government subsidies began to diminish significantly in real terms, so that additional contributions of resources drawn from municipal funds were required. In this sense, rather than reflecting financial autonomy, the evolution of municipal revenues connected with subsidies illustrates the rapid growth in resources raised by the municipalities during this period.

Other transfers from the central government to the municipalities also rose sharply, especially in the second half of the eighties. Thus, while the FNDR soared to nearly five times the 1985 level, other programs in such areas as neighborhood and urban improvement went into operation during this period, generating new resources. Like the education and health subsidies, these funds were directly tied to new spending commitments. Nevertheless, since they were essentially intended for investment, they made it possible to offset the drop in investment with the municipalities' own resources toward the end of the period.

In this way, the resources administered directly or indirectly by the municipalities quadrupled from less than 1 percent of GDP in the mid-seventies in a little over a decade. In 1991 these resources totaled the equivalent of 3.9 percent of GDP and 15 percent of total government

---

[42] The economic growth of the last five years, however, did not have the expected impact on municipal revenues because the use of values obtained from the new property assessments (on which the real estate tax is based) was postponed several times.

Figure 3.1. Chile: Municipal Revenue, 1976-88
(Millions of 1985 pesos)

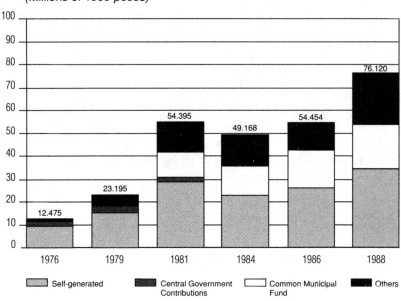

Source: Subsecretariat of Regional Development, Ministry of the Interior.

spending, about the same as one of the major social or infrastructure ministries.[43]

As shown in Table 3.2, however, only half of these resources actually enter the municipal budgets available to the local authorities. Fifty percent of the remaining funds correspond to subsidies for the funding of shifted services, 25 percent to conditioned transfers or to the funding and direct execution of investment for local purposes, and 25 percent to social subsidies that are only *earmarked* by the municipality.

Functions, Funding, and Efficiency

Table 3.3 shows the use of these resources. In 1991 municipal government and the operation of the shifted services each accounted for around

---

[43] It should be noted that these figures correspond to total outlays administered directly or indirectly by the municipalities. Given that only half these outlays are financed with funds put up by the municipalities, the degree of fiscal decentralization measured on the revenue side is smaller than if it were measured from the expenditure standpoint. This distinction is important when making international comparisons.

Table 3.2. Chile: Sources of Municipal Funds in 1991

Sources	Millions of pesos	Percentage of total municipal funds	Percentage of total central govt. spending	Percentage of GNP
I. SELF-GENERATED INCOME*	52.044	12.31	1.98	0.48
I.1. Operating income	27.987	6.62	1.06	0.26
I.1.a. Maintenance fees	4.497	1.06	0.17	0.04
I.2. Other	24.057	5.69	0.91	0.22
II. DUTIES AND FEES*	155.122	36.70	5.89	1.42
II.1. Property taxes	77.621	18.37	2.95	0.71
II.2. Permits	24.841	5.88	0.94	0.23
II.3. Automobile registration	27.653	6.54	1.05	0.25
II.4. Other duties and fees (a)	17.722	4.19	0.67	0.16
II.5. Interest and penalties	7.285	1.72	0.28	0.07
III. TRANSFERS FROM THE CENTRAL GOVERNMENT*	165.362	39.13	6.28	1.51
III.1. Ordinary funds for education and health (b)	122.692	29.03	4.66	1.12
III.2. Extraordinary funding (c)	1.307	0.31	0.05	0.01
III.3. Financing of investments (d)	41.363	9.79	1.57	0.38
IV. THIRD-PARTY FUNDING**	50.105	11.86	1.90	0.46
IV.1. Social subsidies (e)	46.788	11.07	1.78	0.43
IV.2. Other social programs (f)	0.727	0.17	0.03	0.01
IV.3. Agreements (g)	2.590	0.61	0.10	0.02
V. BUDGETARY RESOURCES (I+II+III.1+III.2)	331.165	78.36	12.57	3.03
VI. RESOURCES OUTSIDE THE BUDGET (III.3+IV)	91.468	21.64	3.47	0.84
TOTAL	422.633	100.00	16.04	3.86

Source: Author's calculations based on figures from the Budget Office, Ministry of the Economy.
Notes:
(a) Includes mineral rights of municipal benefit.
(b) Includes contributions for the financing of the educational by-laws.
(c) Includes extraordinary contributions for education and tax surcharges on residential real estate.
(d) Includes FNDR (education, health, and other investments of municipal benefit), neighborhood improvement programs, urban improvement, and ISAR.
(e) SUF, PASIS, and a subsidy for the consumption of drinking water.
(f) Includes transfers from DIGEDER and the Social Fund.
(g) There currently exist transfers to municipalities for agreement programs in the following services: Ministry of Agriculture, Ministry of Labor (youth training program), Ministry of Health (alcohol treatment centers and mental health facilities), MIDEPLAN, SERNAN, and INJ.
* In the municipal budget performance.
** In the budget performance of the central government.

Table 3.3. Chile: Use of Municipal Resources in 1991

Uses	Millions of pesos	Percentage of total municipal resources	Percentage of central govt. spending	Percentage of GNP
I. MUNICIPAL MANAGEMENT*	168.280	41.55	6.39	1.54
I.1. Current expenditures	145.518	35.93	5.52	1.33
I.1.a. Personnel	33.408	8.25	1.27	0.31
I.1.b. Goods and services	70.014	17.29	2.66	0.64
I.1.c. Current transfers	15.266	3.77	0.58	0.14
I.1.d. Other	26.830	6.62	1.02	0.25
I.2. Capital expenditures	22.762	5.62	0.86	0.21
I.2.a. Real investment	22.762	5.62	0.86	0.21
I.2.b. Other	0	0.00	0.00	0.00
II. TRANSFERRED SERVICES*(a)	161.222	39.81	6.12	1.47
II.1. Education	132.903	32.82	5.05	1.21
II.1.a. Operation	123.192	30.42	4.68	1.13
II.1.b. Investments (b)	9.711	2.40	0.37	0.09
II.2. Health and other	28.319	6.99	1.08	0.26
II.2.a. Operation	20.397	5.04	0.77	0.19
II.2.b. Investments(b)	7.922	1.96	0.30	0.07
III. CENTRAL GOVT. PROGRAMS**	73.838	18.23	2.80	0.67
III.1. FNDR-Infrastructure(c)	4.304	1.06	0.16	0.04
III.2. Neighborhood improvement	15.047	3.72	0.57	0.14
III.3. Urban improvement	4.382	1.08	0.17	0.04
III.4. Monetary subsidies	46.788	11.55	1.78	0.43
III.5. Other	3.317	0.82	0.13	0.03
IV. OTHER	1.663	0.41	0.06	0.02
TOTAL	405.003	100.00	15.38	3.70

Source: Author's calculations based on figures from the Budget Office, Ministry of the Economy.
(a) Includes services transferred to corporations.
(b) Sectoral components of the FNDR.
(c) The remainder from FNDR.
(d) There currently exist transfers to municipalities for agreement programs in the following services: Ministry of Agriculture, Ministry of Labor (youth training program), Ministry of Health (alcohol treatment centers and mental health facilities), MIDEPLAN, SERNAN, and INJ.
* In the municipal budget performance.
** In the budget performance of the central government.

40 percent of all uses, with the remaining 18 percent devoted to programs delegated by the central government.

Table 3.4 shows, from a more conceptual and detailed point of view, the structure of responsibilities and municipal financing to which the Chilean reforms are giving rise. This table seeks to facilitate comparison with the optimal municipal structure previously outlined and sum-

Table 3.4. Municipal Functions and Sources of Financing in Chile

Function		Financing	
General category	Specific functions	General category	Specific sources
General administration	Municipal operations Promotion and regulation of community activities	Taxes and operating income	Property taxes
Urban regulation	Regulation of construction, transit, and transport		Vehicle registration fees
	Urban planning		Commercial and professional licenses Other operating income Common Municipal Fund
Provision of public goods and services	Prevention of risks and emergencies Environmental protection Street cleaning Park and garden maintenance Sewage		
	Public lighting		
	Garbage collection	User fees	Direct charges
Investment in infrastructure	Road construction and repair Construction of infrastructure	Closed transfers without co- financing	Self-generated resources Program of Urban Improvement Housing and public works
Social services	Promotion of employment and training		Transfers from DIGEDER
	Sports and recreation Social assistance Administration of schools Administration of health services	Open transfers without co- financing	Social Fund FOSIS Educational subsidies Subsidies from the Ministry of Health (FAPEM)
	Construction of public housing and core sanitation	Debt	Neighborhood improvement programs
	Allocation of monetary subsidies	External funds	Public Treasury

marized in Table 3.1, so as to evaluate the degree of economic efficiency that the Chilean decentralization model would make possible. For this purpose the more detailed functions and sources of municipal revenues are identified in the two end columns of Table 3.4, with the subject categories used previously.

The area of authority assumed by Chilean municipalities is extraordinarily broad, encompassing all matters in which local management offers comparative advantages. Especially important in this respect are the social services, in which the municipalities have a hand in practically all areas of social policy, with the justifiable exception of social security.

Funding sources are less diversified than municipal functions. Funding is concentrated almost exclusively in tax sources and in transfers from the central government. User fees, though important in increasing municipal revenue in the eighties, are limited to garbage collection, in which cost recovery is partial. Borrowing is negligible.[44]

Table 3.4 shows that the ratio between municipal revenue and functions in Chile is not inconsistent with recommendations based on economic efficiency criteria, which show some sizable gaps. Operational and tax revenues finance the regular operation of the municipalities and the provision of public goods, inasmuch as an appreciable share of the investments operates on the basis of transfers. The limitations are due to relatively limited use of cost recovery, the restricted opportunity for local choice with respect to the level and distribution of the municipalities' own revenues, and the overwhelming prevalence of transfers without counterpart. As we shall see further on, such transfers have affected the incentives under which the municipalities operate.

In this way, the Chilean decentralization model approximates, in general terms, the ideal structure of functions and funding that— theoretically—maximizes economic efficiency. Nonetheless, the materialization of these advantages is still limited by institutional, financial, and administrative factors. To paraphrase a recent World Bank report, the challenge is to transform the theoretical benefits of decentralization into real benefits while avoiding undue loss of efficiency and quality in the services.[45] These challenges are examined in the next section.

Aspects of Municipal Development in Chile

All real decentralization experiences have three elements in common: (1) they are essentially political processes, since they have to do with the dis-

---

[44] The only recorded instance of borrowing is for the neighborhood improvement program, in which the municipalities are supposed to recover part of housing construction costs from the recipients. In practice, however, this recovery has been very low, and the municipalities have had to resort to simplified, very partial payment systems.

[45] World Bank (1992).

tribution of power within the state; (2) they require changes in the management and organizational culture of state institutions; and (3) they have to do with resources, whether in terms of sharing the taxing authority of the central government or because the imbalances between municipal functions and their financing force the establishment of intragovernmental resource transfers.[46]

The foregoing boils down to saying that all decentralization processes involve a certain amount of conflict. However, such conflict often springs from contradictions between the objectives and the instruments of decentralization. A swift transfer of functions from the central government based on political considerations can soon encounter limitations in the administrative capacity of the municipalities; direct control of municipal financing by the central government can weaken incentives for efficient management; shifting resources without responsibilities affects public finance, and so on. By and large it can therefore be said that successful decentralization depends on the ability to resolve the conflicts that arise while the decentralization is being implemented.

This section examines the chief topics growing out of the Chilean municipal experience in each of the three areas mentioned.

Institutional Aspects

Scope of Municipal Functions. The functions of municipalities in Chile are many, involving in particular administration, urban improvement, and social affairs.[47] These functions, however, derive not from broadly defined powers but from a detailed list contained in the Organic Constitutional Law on Municipalities. Some authors have commented that this approach derives from the Chilean centralizing tradition and from mistrust of the state on the part of the military regime that introduced these rules. A proposed alternative is that municipal authority be extended to everything not expressly barred by the law, in the continental European tradition.[48]

To switch from a restrictive to an unrestrictive definition of municipal authority inevitably enlarges the municipalities' field of action, opening up new areas to local elective office and making the system more flexible. Still, this approach is not without difficulties. To begin with, it

---

[46] Bird (1990), p. 278.
[47] For a complete analysis of the functions of Chilean municipalities, see World Bank (1992), Chapter 2.
[48] Fuentes (1992), p. 194.

does not seem wise to diversify municipal endeavors at a stage when the present functions are still not being carried out satisfactorily. Further, it is highly probable that under those circumstances functions will be duplicated in the public sector. Finally, it is not clear that municipal action will be made more efficient by giving communities more tasks to choose from, for the process may become too complex for voters to understand. If the object is to let the municipalities decide more matters for themselves, it would be preferable to start in areas already subject to local government in which too many constraints are still present. From that perspective, a restrictive definition of municipal functions may prove helpful in guiding the decentralization process by forcing the division of responsibilities between the different levels of government to be defined more clearly.

Regional Government Functions. A similar problem of definition of authority has arisen with the creation of the regional governments. At the general level, the constitutional reform of 1992 determined that they would act on investment, encouragement of production, and social development. In the case of the last two items, however, certain limitations have been placed on power and authority in the face of regional demands for greater freedom of action.

The prioritization—as well as limitation—of regional government functions in Chile is an essential topic for the future of decentralization, especially in the areas mentioned. Actual discussion of these reforms has revealed that the drive for regional autonomy and the pressure to devote more resources to the regions are powerful factors in this process. In this light, the regional governments can either exercise autonomy by taking decisions on a number of issues or become means for the regions to exert pressure on the center.

Under present circumstances in Chile, the first course appears more appropriate. Public investment is an area in which the roles of the three levels of government—national, regional, and local—can be coordinated, given the existence of different categories of investment with respect to which comparative advantages in decision making vary considerably. Extending the authority of regional government to other areas in which municipal authority is already well established, particularly with respect to social issues, can only multiply conflicts of authority and bureaucracy without advancing decentralization or government efficiency.

Social Functions. The social sphere has become a privileged area of municipal action. In varying degrees, municipalities have taken over a number of responsibilities and tasks with results that would have been difficult to foresee only a few years ago. This success is partly due to the growing complexity and specificity of government programs in this field.

After the extension of the coverage of the main social programs until the early seventies, in which the goal was to make previously excluded groups eligible for standard benefits, more recent years have seen the emphasis shift to a more intensive social policy. This strategy reflects a special concern with improving the quality of traditional social services and with replacing cash welfare by programs that create opportunities for marginal or vulnerable groups.[49]

This type of program requires a degree of flexibility and specificity difficult to attain in central government agencies. Two important avenues for decentralized action have thus been opened: (1) the administration of small units providing standardized social services, and (2) the implementation of social projects focusing on vulnerable groups.

Chilean practice, initially focused on the first type of effort, has gradually moved toward the second. As a consequence, municipalities have begun to compete with nongovernmental organizations and other public institutions for the funding of social projects through various programs in which the central government essentially plays a financial role.[50]

Unlike conventional schemes for making transfers to municipalities, however, these initiatives entail a greater degree of competition in the allocation of resources among diversified agents and looser political ties between the municipalities and the central government. The stage is thus set for transfers without cofinancing, which avoid the inefficiencies common to such schemes.

Democracy, Governance, and Efficiency. Analysis of the Chilean decentralization experience has traditionally focused on the formal and operational aspects of reforms carried out in the eighties. Many studies, however, have overlooked the peculiar political conditions under which this process took place.[51] The centralized appointment of mayors, the authoritarian administration of the municipalities, and the pronounced dependence of local government on central government policy are not minor or secondary aspects of this experience. In fact, as we saw earlier, it can be argued that quite a few of the advantages of decentralization in

---

[49] See Marcel and Solimano (1993).

[50] This is the case, for example, with the programs to finance social projects administered by the Solidarity and Social Investment Fund (FOSIS) and the national Youth Job Training Program.

[51] See the recommendations in Campbell (1991), pp. 19–21.

terms of efficiency are determined by the possibilities of collective election at the local level. If such possibilities are negated by a surfeit of authoritarian control and if, further, fiscal authority is very restricted, then it cannot be maintained that decentralization is contributing to economic efficiency.

The evidence is rather clear that the previous administration's goal was not exactly to increase efficiency by this method. Under the approach to intergovernmental relations imposed during this stage of the reform process, the municipalities were seen more as agents of the central government than as autonomous entities with the power to make decisions and allocate resources.

Accordingly, the democratization of the municipalities under the current administration can be regarded as a contribution to the economic efficiency of the democratization process in Chile. Still, local democracy is much more than the election of mayors and council members by popular vote. The lasting establishment of local democracy and its contribution to achieving greater consistency between community preferences and the services provided by the municipalities require that two conditions be met. The first is that more choices be made locally, as is already proposed, for example, with respect to the setting of the real estate tax. That of course entails adopting an approach closer to local choice in the decentralization process. A second requirement for improving efficiency in the decentralization process is to strengthen government at the local level. The community has to be able to express its preferences during the decision-making process and to evaluate the results. Tools such as annual plans, public hearings, and progress reports are fundamental in that respect.[52]

Economic and Social Structure and Decentralization. The actual execution of decentralization is closely determined by political and administrative circumscriptions. In general, the economic analysis of decentralization assumes the existence of jurisdiction over relatively small, homogeneous communes with some tax base.

In Chile there are currently 334 communes. Of these, 16 were created in the last decade, most of them in the Santiago metropolitan region. The present structure of the communes, and especially that of recent subdivisions, shows that the dominant concern was to prevent the

---

[52] This criterion was reinforced in the city of Santiago with the marked trend toward social segregation manifested under the military government. This process is fundamentally tied to the eradication policy, which called for transferring marginal populations from various districts of the city to the south and west sections.

existence of excessively large communes and to ensure a certain degree of socioeconomic homogeneity within the communes.[53] The result of this policy is an enormous economic and social heterogeneity. At present 200 communes have fewer than 20,000 inhabitants, with 15 percent of the country's total population, while at the other end 40 municipalities, with more than 100,000 inhabitants each, absorb 57 percent of the population.[54] These municipalities furthermore contain more than half the country's poor. The tax base is also heavily concentrated, especially because of real estate tax exemptions.

Apparently, the subdivision policy followed by the military government rested on the conviction that greater socioeconomic uniformity in the communes would help the redistributive effect of the Municipal Common Fund and the government transfer programs. The practical effect, however, was to make the revenues of a large proportion of the municipalities almost exclusively dependent on contributions received from the Municipal Common Fund, with no prospect of generating sizable revenues of their own. Under those circumstances choice is out of the question because the direction in which incentives operate on the municipal authorities is doubtful.[55]

If municipal governments with greater autonomy are to be created in Chile, communal boundaries will have to be defined in a manner more consistent with that goal. Although this is a politically complex process, there are countries that have carried out this type of municipal regrouping.

Financial Aspects

Level of Municipal Revenues. The previous section dealt with the history of municipal revenue through the 1980s. The conclusion was that revenues were affected by the stimulus arising when the municipal revenues law went into effect, first by the 1982–83 recession and subsequently by the postponement in incorporating new property assessments into taxes on real estate. In the same period, however, municipal expenditures did not follow the same course. The need to cover shortfalls from the shifted educational and health services was added to the requirements associated with population growth, expanding economic activity,

---

[53] World Bank (1992), p. 11.

[54] On this subject, see Tomic and González (1983), pp. 54–55.

[55] Permanent self-generated revenues include returns on investment, the real estate tax, receipts for driver's permits (automobile tax), municipal licenses, fees for garbage collection and other services, fines, and interest.

Figure 3.2. Chile: Permanent Municipal Budget Shortfall
(Millions of December 1991 pesos)

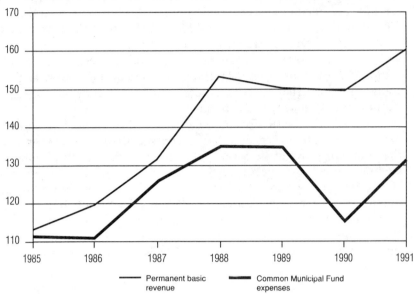

Source: Author's calculations based on figures from the Subsecretariat of Regional Development, Ministry of the Interior.

and growing urbanization. As shown by Figure 3.2, this meant that the available portion of permanent basic revenues (deducted from the contributions for education and health) no longer sufficed for the purpose of funding the municipalities' regular operating costs, and the gap was filled by cuts in municipal investment, one-time earnings such as proceeds from the sale of assets, and central government inputs through the Municipal Common Fund.[56]

This situation will be difficult to sustain in the future. Sound financial administration requires raising the municipalities' own revenues *permanently*. There are two alternative methods to attain that end: (1) allow the new property assessments to take effect, thereby increasing revenue through the real estate tax, and (2) raise the local tax burden.

The most obvious alternative for raising local taxes is the real estate tax. This tax is not only the most important in terms of receipts—it

---

[56] Permanent basic revenues correspond to the receipts from a surtax on urban properties over a certain value, introduced in 1985 with fiscal benefit. Exemptions are so numerous that a complete annex to the real estate tax law was required to record them.

accounts for around one-third of the municipalities' own revenues—but the evidence is that its tax impact is moderate. In effect, the real estate tax currently accounts for around 0.5 percent of GDP, part of which is a fiscal revenue, and it is deductible from business income tax. This low significance is commensurate with the range of real estate tax exemptions as well as the underestimation of property values. It is estimated that in Chile 60 percent of property value is exempt, either because it is below the taxable minimum—as in the case of urban properties—or because of special provisions accumulated over the years.[57] A review of these exemptions would not only make it possible to raise municipal revenues but would also make the tax more rational. Fear of resistance from currently exempted taxpayers should be countered by noting that, with respect to the general exemption on residential properties, the tax applies a flat rate to the nonexempt portion of these properties and therefore its effect would be identical on all taxpayers over the new exempt minimum.

Flexibility in the Tax System. One of the great limitations of the municipal model developed by the military government was the rigidity of the municipal tax system. As this system was based on centrally set flat rates, one of the most important areas of choice was eliminated. This also prevented residents of communes from knowing the cost of their preferences and reaching decisions accordingly.

Complete flexibility in local taxation is not desirable either. The initially immovable factors justifying the rationality of taxing property at the local level can become movable in the presence of a system of high and strongly differentiated tax rates. From the economic point of view, the effect of these differences on citizens' decisions works against efficiency in resource allocation.

In cases like that of Chile, there is a further argument against extreme flexibility in the matter of real estate tax. Where a relatively high exempt minimum property value exists and the tax base is distributed in very unequal fashion, it cannot be assumed that collective decisions on the tax rate will affect the residents of the community equally. It seems more probable that a majority of the local population would approve taxes that fall on a minority of the taxpayers.

Consequently it would seem appropriate to adopt a scheme combining (1) autonomy in setting the tax rate within a "band" containing

---

[57] The potential of this type of tax exemptions to foster housing construction is debatable, with empirical evidence pointing to different conclusions. See Bahl and Linn (1992), chapters 5 and 6.

the general tax,[58] and (2) reduced exemptions with a broader tax base and a larger taxpaying population.

Joint Tax Administration. Real estate tax is defined in Chile as a national tax for municipal benefit. That means, among other things, that the principal decisions on exemptions, bases, and rates are made by the central government, which, moreover, administers the tax. This latter aspect has given rise to many a discussion in Chile, with inconclusive results.[59] Less discussed, but fully documented in works published on other countries, have been the political consequences of maintaining central decision-making power over taxation.[60]

In Chile these problems have recently come to the fore with respect to property assessments. In fact, public protests during this process prompted the central government to postpone the application of those assessments a number of times. The municipalities have been the ones to bear the cost of the postponements. This is a much greater and deeper problem than those concerning possible administrative difficulties.

This experience adds a new argument in favor of a flexible rate system that when flexibility is permitted at the local level, many of the immediate problems of implementing the new assessments can be absorbed and resolved at that level without exposing the central government to major stress. The next advisable step, however, would be to render the assessment process less volatile by updating it with greater frequency and better timing.

Municipal Common Fund. The Municipal Common Fund is not only openly redistributive in purpose but also considered one of the main components of municipal reform.[61] Nevertheless, it is not clear what the

---

[58] Other topics relating to a flexible real estate tax refer to the definition of inputs from this source, the Municipal Common Fund, and the possibility of flexible exemptions. See World Bank (1992), chapter 3.

[59] For a presentation of the arguments in favor of shifting more responsibility for administering the real estate tax to the municipalities, see the articles in Irarrázabal (1992).

[60] Bahl and Linn (1992), chapter 4.

[61] The Municipal Social Fund is a redistributive fund of municipal resources maintained by a fraction of municipal tax receipts prorated on actual receipts. It is distributed in accordance with a set of indicators. Contributions to the fund consist of: (1) 60 percent of real estate taxes; (2) 50 percent of the fees for vehicular traffic permits; and (3) a fraction of the fees for municipal licenses charged by the three richest communes. Its resources are distributed in accordance with the following formula: (1) 10 percent as an absolutely equal amount; (2) 20 percent in proportion to the population of the commune; (3) 30 percent in proportion to exempt properties in the commune with respect to the country's total

criterion guiding the redistribution is. As noted in the second section above, a desirable criterion would be to ensure a minimum level of fiscal equity within the municipal funding system. This criterion is best satisfied when resources are distributed in such a way as to compensate for (1) inadequate tax bases and (2) spending above the average. As in the Chilean case, this approach is more effective when municipal resources are redistributed than when transfers from the central government are distributed.

How does the Municipal Common Fund's formula compare with this approach? The inadequacy of the tax base seems to be satisfactorily picked up in the indicator of smaller permanent municipal revenues. However, two important reservations remain. In the first place, the Chilean formula is based on actual collection, thus including the incidence of tax evasion. In the second place, the effect of the real estate tax exemptions appears aggravated inasmuch as this tax is not only a determinant of the municipalities' own permanent revenues but is included as an additional indicator for the distribution of resources, heavily weighted (30 percent). That presents a twofold problem: the same indicator is counted twice, but a variable over which the municipalities have some control is especially weighted, which gives rise to moral risk problems.[62]

With respect to costs, the indicators used in the Municipal Common Fund formula are especially deficient as they cover only population and exempted properties (if the latter indicator is taken as a substitute for poverty). Ways can be devised to improve this formula. To do so, it would be necessary to analyze in some detail the main exogenous determinants of the municipalities' operating costs and work those determinants into the formula.

Transfers from the Central Government. As was mentioned previously, transfers from the central government have constituted the most dynamic component of municipal financing in recent years.[63] As shown in Table 3.5 and Figure 3.3, such transfers, excluding subsidies for edu-

---

exempt properties; and (4) 40 percent in proportion to the municipalities' own smaller permanent revenues with respect to the national average. For an in-depth analysis of the fund's operation, see Ministry of the Interior (1992), pp. 56–58; Bravo (1992); and World Bank (1992), Chapter 3.

[62] This is due to the fact that the municipalities may not only apply to the central government for special exemptions within their jurisdictions, but they can alter the housing exemptions by redefining their urban boundaries. The problem noted in the text is therefore a special reason to deny the municipalities autonomy in the matter of exemptions.

[63] Irarrázabal and Joannon (1992).

Table 3.5. Chile: Free Transfers to the Municipalities[a]
(Millions of 1992 pesos)

	1987	1992	Var %
Investment	33.731	53.047	57.3
Subsidies	26.122	55.674	113.1
Others[b]	12.281	16.357	33.2
Total	72.134	125.078	73.4
Transfers/Income (%)	61.0	70.4	

Source: Ministry of the Interior.
Notes:
[a] Excludes contributions for education and health.
[b] Includes contributions for the deficit.

cation and health, grew 73.4 percent in real terms from 1987 to 1992, and from 61 percent to 70 percent as a share of the municipalities' own permanent revenues. The growth of these transfers is linked both to the creation of new programs and to the expansion of existing ones.

Transfers to municipalities take one of only two forms in Chile: allocated or unallocated conditioned transfers, without cofinancing. The cofinanced transfers or tax-sharing arrangements often found in other Latin American countries do not exist.[64]

The growing importance of transfers and the preference for methods that require a low degree of municipal financial commitment are introducing substantial distortions into decision making at the local level. As noted by the World Bank (1992), in this case the local authorities have an incentive to maximize their demands for capital financing at the cost of central government finances. No rationing of projects is based on cost factors.[65] An additional distortion stems from underestimation of recurrent costs when local investment projects are analyzed.

The solution to these distortions is to introduce a greater degree of local involvement in investments. All these cases entail projects that largely benefit the local community itself, so that such a change would, moreover, help to make resource allocation more efficient. Given the starting point, however, the municipalities must concurrently develop mechanisms to recover capital costs if increased cofinancing of projects is to be viable and equitable.

---

[64] The recent changes in the mining license regime constitute an exception. Mining licenses have changed from qualifying as a tax exemption to being shared by regional governments and municipalities.
[65] World Bank (1992), p. xii.

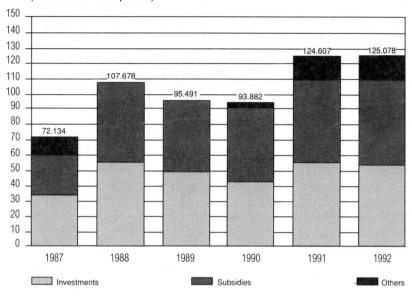

Figure 3.3. Chile: Transfers to Municipalities
(Millions of 1992 pesos)

Investments — Subsidies — Others

Source: Ministry of the Interior.

Borrowing. Borrowing is a potential alternative funding source for municipal investment. This mechanism shares with cofinancing systems the advantage of committing the municipalities' own resources, thus encouraging rational investment programming and resource allocation.

In Chile, municipalities may not borrow.[66] This limitation has an essentially fiscal rationale: the risk of losing control over public finances when a sector can go into debt without obeying the financial authority's guidelines. Some authors have argued that the scale of operations of the municipal sector would preclude this sector from originating significant imbalances from the fiscal point of view.[67] This argument, however, must carry little weight with authorities coping with the daily pressures of a host of government agencies, each of which, considered individually, is small when set next to the total fiscal aggregates.

---

[66] Borrowing is not strictly prohibited, but a special law has to authorize each loan. With this restriction, it is not surprising that only two such operations have been recorded in the last 15 years. Both had negative results.

[67] Bird (1990).

The limitation on borrowing, however, is a problem that affects municipal government by preventing the efficient management of local finances and shortening programming horizons, introducing uncertainty, and fueling excessive demand for transfers. These problems are so pressing that Chilean municipalities have resorted to indirect borrowing, such as leasing equipment and delaying social security payments.

Are there therefore no alternatives that would allow a prudent use of borrowing by the municipalities without eroding fiscal discipline? A sensitive strategy in this respect ought to include at least three elements: (1) making the authorities more directly responsible for their borrowing decisions;[68] (2) enhancing the cost recovery mechanisms, in accordance with the previous point; and (3) establishing a system for guiding the decisions of lending agencies with respect to borrowing by municipalities. Concerning this last point, financial discipline at the local level would be well served by subjecting the municipalities to a financial "qualification" system similar to those in place in countries with a higher degree of municipal autonomy.[69]

Financing Shifted Services. Economic works on decentralization conclude that a system of open transfers without cofinancing, such as the system in effect in Chile, is the best approach to the financing of services with major externalities and minimum quality standards when management of those standards is turned over to the municipalities by reason of their administrative advantages. Those transfers should be determined on the basis of a standard unit cost per benefit.

Less obvious, however, is the manner in which that standard cost can be determined in the case of such services as education and health, in which more than 80 percent of operating costs stem from remunerations. In this case, any evaluation of the amount of those transfers turns into an analysis of personnel compensation, and vice versa. This direct relationship, obvious to those involved, compromises the viability of an effective

---

[68] A move in this direction has already been made by the recent establishment of the joint responsibility of council members in the approval of properly balanced budgets. On this point, see Ministry of the Interior (1992), pp. 51–52.

[69] A municipal bond market, for example, can encourage better financial management. Municipalities with higher credit ratings could obtain more funding at lower cost than those considered high-risk, and star performers could generate a more direct and measurable benefit than when borrowing is executed through the central government. However, the development of a market with these characteristics in Chile would require substantial changes in the structure of the capital market and in intragovernmental financial and political relations.

decentralization of these functions, since the pressures of instructors and health personnel, sometimes with the support of the municipal authorities themselves, bear directly on the central government. The government's reaction to these pressures can in turn limit the municipal autonomy that motivates the shifting of these functions in the first place.

This situation gives rise to two alternative strategies. First, in order to maintain a system of delegated administration for social services that are cost-intensive due to personnel costs, it is essential to prevent inflexibility in hiring decisions, for in that case compensation is left as the only adjustable variable in the entire system. Second, subsidy transfer mechanisms should be reviewed with the aim of avoiding a direct link with compensation. An alternative is to merge specific transfers for education and health into a general transfer that would include the same indicators as those used for the distribution of the specific transfers, perhaps in the form of a fiscal contribution to the Municipal Common Fund. In this approach the resources would be incorporated into a more flexible fund for use without reducing the overall volume of each municipality. A further consequence of opting for this approach would be to avoid the popular interpretation of any municipal contribution to education or health as a "deficit."

Educational Subsidies. Chile's system of educational subsidies per student has been praised for its rationality and efficiency. This approach, which leaves families free to choose the school (municipal or subsidized private) to which they send their children, couples efficient use of public resources with a powerful incentive to improve the quality of education. Here, however, theory contrasts with the fact of a spreading perception that the quality of Chilean education has been deteriorating in the last few years.

The explanation of this paradox may lie in the true role that the quality of education plays in the market created by the subsidy system. In evaluating this role, one should note that few variables are more difficult for families to measure than the quality of their children's education, especially in the short term. Other aspects of the school system—school infrastructure, teacher qualifications, discipline—are much more obvious. Evidence exists that these other considerations have been the chief factors guiding the decisions of the Chilean public in recent years. If those factors are not very strongly linked to educational quality, then the subsidy system does not ensure improved quality and a gain for the students.

For the families, the problem of educational quality is essentially one of information. In this respect the sectoral authorities can do a great deal in Chile, and a universal system for measuring educational quality, known by the acronym SIMCE, has been in use for several years.[70] Public disclosure of the results of SIMCE for each school—perhaps standardized according to student characteristics—would help guide families in making decisions and would improve efficiency in the subsidy system.

Administrative Aspects

Personnel Administration. Personnel administration is a fundamental determinant of the management of public agencies. Any reform process that attempts to ensure that the shift of responsibilities to the municipalities is accompanied by a parallel advance in local management capacity must pay special attention to this point. The upgrading and professionalization of the municipalities and the creation of incentives will improve personnel performance and form an important element of any strategy in this area.

Some authors have suggested that progress in decentralization would be based partly on the military government's efforts in this field. In this respect, to paraphrase Campbell, Chilean efforts at reinforcement begun in the early 1970s—consisting of modifications of the civil service, career ladders, and salary reforms for municipal workers—make the most typical component of World Bank institution-building projects look anemic by comparison.[71]

Castañeda (1990) presents evidence of important changes in the composition of municipal personnel whereby the proportion of professional and technical staff has risen from 7.9 percent of the total in 1975 to almost a third in 1988.[72]

Much of the available information, however, tends to qualify these enthusiastic appraisals. In the first place, the figures on the composition of municipal personnel are subject to the following factors: (1) cuts in nonprofessional staff (accompanied by layoffs) by subcontracting services such as garbage collection to the private sector; (2) shifts of professionals and technicians from the central government to the administration of the

---

[70] SIMCE (Sistema de Medición de la Calidad de la Educación [Education Quality Measuring System]) consists of an annual examination applied alternately to the fourth and eighth grades of all primary and secondary schools (municipal, subsidized private, and paid private) throughout the country. This examination is designed to gauge success in achieving educational objectives and also includes a questionnaire intended to obtain a more qualitative evaluation of how students relate to their environment.

[71] Campbell (1991), p. 52.

[72] Castañeda (1990), p. 300.

taxes and fees to be paid to the municipalities; and (3) conversion of administrative to technical positions based on acknowledgement of staff members' earlier qualifications. If these factors are taken into account, it transpires that no extraordinary upgrading of municipal personnel took place but that this sector followed the same gradual process of professionalization that occurred in the central government.[73] In any case, in 1991 the municipalities' staffing structure was still considerably less professionalized than that of the central government. As Table 3.6 shows, professionals and technicians made up about a quarter of all municipal personnel as against 50 percent of central government personnel. Other salient features of the municipal sector are that it has a higher proportion of men and young workers.

In the second place, the apparent improvement in the compensation of municipal professionals and technicians referred to in the studies cited had only a partial compensatory effect, which was soon overtaken by the sharp drop in real civil service pay during the eighties. That drop opened a substantial gap compared to the private sector, which, under the current conditions of low unemployment, has seriously affected public management.

In the third place, the military government adopted a number of measures that made personnel administration in the municipal sector more rather than less difficult. These measures included: (1) arbitrary staffing patterns; (2) favoritism in the appointment and promotion of officials and arbitrariness in dismissals; (3) the replacement, in the final days of military government, of freedom to dismiss by a freeze on dismissals; (4) the introduction of severe rigidities such as the prohibition on short-term contracts; and (5) the destruction of any career prospects.[74]

It is therefore possible that, as the authors quoted state, the Chilean municipal sector is one of the most professionalized in the hemisphere and that it deserves much of the praise for the success of the reform process. Nevertheless, the foregoing leads us to conclude that this success was achieved more in spite of personnel administration under the former government than because of it. This conclusion in turn suggests that the upgrading and modernization of municipal personnel currently under-way may significantly further the decentralization process.

---

[73] In fact, the composition of municipal personnel indicated by Castañeda coincides approximately with the composition of central government personnel at the present time.
[74] An indicator of the existence of such prospects during the previous regime is the fact that at the beginning of the nineties a large proportion of municipal employees had not had promotions since 1981.

Table 3.6. Chile: Composition of Personnel in the Municipalities and the Central Government, 1991
(Percentages)

	Municipalities	Central government
BY LEVEL		
Managers and directors	6.4	6.5
Professionals and technicians	25.6	50.4
Administrative and support staff	68.0	43.1
BY GENDER		
Male	65.7	39.8
Female	34.3	60.2
BY AGE		
Under 34 yrs. old	34.3	28.9
34–59 yrs. old	59.2	63.8
60 yrs. and older	6.4	7.4

Source: Office of the Budget, Ministry of the Economy.

Improving Management. The economic analysis of decentralization implicitly assumes local competence comparable, at the least, with that of the central government. That is generally not the case in Chile. The municipalities are often seen as a lower level of public administration and as a lower rung of a career ladder. In such a setting it is not surprising to find the development of modern public management techniques lagging even more than in the central government.

Beyond the personnel administration problems noted above, the municipalities display serious shortcomings in financial management, investment programming, social planning, and so on. In addition to the development of incentives to encourage better local management, fully discussed in this document, the need in Chile is for a planned and systematic effort to raise the quality of management in each of these areas. That effort should provide for the adaptation of modern financial and administrative tools such as multiannual budgets, the application of management information systems, cost-center accounting, and investment programming.[75]

This effort would, however, make little sense if the problem of the municipalities' organizational culture is not dealt with seriously. Some basic elements of this culture are shared with the central administration:

---

[75] World Bank (1992), Chapter 5.

ex ante control, concentration of responsibilities, and a conservative attitude. What is specific to the municipal sector, however, is centralism. If the economic success of decentralization depends, as this document maintains, on the steady creation of areas of autonomous local action, then such autonomy must be extended to the internal management of the municipalities, letting them assume responsibility for projects and resources, evaluate working groups, and reward good performance.

Comments

Decentralization is regarded by economists as a determinant of efficiency in the economic management of the state. The reason is that shifting the power to make decisions to the local level allows better adaptation of services offered by the state to the needs and priorities of the community. In that way, decentralization is conducive to economic efficiency insofar as (1) it is accompanied by mechanisms of governance at the local level, and (2) it offers growing areas of flexibility and autonomy to subnational governments.

Municipal decentralization in Chile was initially based on an approach that, rather than shifting decision-making power to the municipalities, sought to use them and develop their role as administrative, economic, and political agents of the central government. That was evidenced by, among other things, the shifting of packages of responsibilities and resources in the social sphere and by the intensive use of unilateral transfers as a mechanism for funding local investments.

The reforms necessary to carry out this process were profound, drastically changing the institutional and financial profile of municipalities in Chile. However, the real decentralization process was not free from operational problems. Those problems derive from the difficulty in matching the shifting of responsibilities from the central government with the abilities and available facilities of the municipalities. As a result, by the end of the eighties some essential elements of the prevailing decentralization model were being strongly questioned by sizable sectors of the community.

In recent years, decentralization has received fresh impetus in Chile. This impetus has not only confirmed the shifting of educational and health services to the municipalities under the new political conditions, but has also brought constitutional and legal reforms providing for the democratic election of municipal authorities and the setting up of regional governments.

The democratization of the municipalities calls for a definitive choice concerning the decentralization model to be followed in the future. One alternative is to pursue their role as agents of the central government, which would require perfecting the existing transfer systems and control mechanisms. The other is for the country to turn progressively toward greater autonomy and local decision making, thus maximizing economic efficiency.

Three requirements are fundamental to the success of a decentralization model based on local autonomy and decision making. The first is to improve decision and control mechanisms. Democratic designation of municipal authorities is a necessary but insufficient condition for letting the community chose among alternative service and funding packages. Therefore, when larger areas of participation in local decision making are created, democracy is strengthened and, moreover, public resource allocation is made more efficient.

A second requirement is to improve methods of generating and allocating resources. A strategy for achieving this goal should include (1) matching the level and distribution of permanent municipal revenues—especially tax revenues—to the routine spending needs attendant upon municipal functions, and (2) substantially improving the system of incentives within which municipalities operate. With respect to this last point, transfers from the central government to fund the shifted education and health services and investments must be perfected.

The third point is that improving municipal management is essential. It is obvious that in Chile the municipalities' technical capacity has not kept pace with their ever more numerous and varied responsibilities. However, the required higher level of competence will not come about spontaneously or through training courses. The need is for a structured management modernization program including among its priorities the improvement of municipal personnel administration and the development of management control and evaluation instruments.

One of the chief lessons taught by the Chilean experience is that progress in decentralization depends on careful coordination of institutional, financial, and managerial changes. The shifting of responsibilities without autonomy limits the efficiency of local government. Low administrative capacity and excessive politicization in the municipalities makes the national authorities reluctant to transfer responsibilities and resources. A coordinated program to develop autonomy, administrative capacity, and decision making at the local level is therefore much more likely to ensure effective decentralization than grandiose institutional reforms.

In practice, decentralization essentially concerns power and resources. Since these are concentrated primarily in the central government, any progress in this matter depends largely on the disposition of the national political and economic authorities. It is usually assumed that these authorities are chiefly interested in maintaining the greatest possible degree of financial and administrative control over the municipalities. This assumption is at odds with the day-to-day reality of government operations. The more discretion is left to the central government, the more exposed it is to pressures from local authorities, parliamentarians and political leaders. The best system for the national authorities is therefore one in which some of the population's more specific problems can be resolved locally.

Consequently, the most sensible decentralization policy seems to be to open up particular areas of local government progressively. In each case, the shifted functions must be linked to choice, autonomy, and competence. This requires a high degree of boldness on the part of the national authorities. This boldness essentially entails accepting the possibility of mistaken decisions at the local level. But acceptance of calculated risks is, after all, part of politics.

References

Arrow, K.J. 1950. A Difficulty in the Concept of Welfare. *Journal of Political Economy* 58: 328–46.

Bahl, R.W., and J.F. Linn. 1992. *Urban Public Finance in Developing Countries.* New York: Oxford University Press.

Bird, R. 1990. Intergovernmental Finance and Local Taxation in Developing Countries: Some Basic Considerations for Reformers. *Public Administration and Development* 10: 277–88.

Borja, J., *et al.* 1987. *Descentralización del Estado, movimiento social y gestión local.* Santiago de Chile: ICI FLACSO, CLACSO.

Bravo, V. 1992. Fundamentos y principios del sistema de financiamiento municipal. In *Problemas y propuestas para el sistema de financiamiento municipal,* ed., I. Irarrázabal. Serie de Documentos de Trabajo N° 176. Santiago de Chile: Centro de Estudios Públicos.

Campbell, T. 1991. Decentralization to Local Government in LAC: National Strategies and Local Response in Planning, Spending and Management. *Regional Studies Program.* Washington, D.C.: The World Bank.

Castañeda, T. 1990. *Para combatir la pobreza. Política social y descentralización en Chile durante los '80.* Santiago de Chile: Centro de Estudios Públicos.

Fuentes, J.M. 1992. Ideas sobre el financiamiento municipal para una reforma más allá de los cambios marginales. In *Problemas y propuestas para el sistema de financiamiento municipal.* See Irarrázabal, 1992.

Irarrázabal, I., ed. 1992. *Problemas y propuestas para el sistema de financiamiento municipal.* Serie de Documentos de Trabajo N° 176. Santiago de Chile: Centro de Estudios Públicos.

—— and P. Joannon. 1992. Recursos externos de repercusión municipal. In *Problemas y propuestas para el sistema de financiamiento municipal.* See Irarrázabal, 1992.

Marcel, M., and A. Solimano. 1993. Developmentalism, Socialism and Free Market Reform: Three Decades of Income Distribution in Chile. Paper presented at the conference The Chilean Economy: Policy Lessons and Challenges. The Brookings Institution, Washington, D.C.

Ministry of the Interior, Chile. 1992. *Manual de gestión municipal.* Santiago de Chile.

Musgrave, R. 1959. *The Theory of Public Finance: A Study of Public Economy.* New York: McGraw-Hill.

Oates, W. 1972. *Fiscal Federalism.* New York: Harcourt Brace Jovanovich.

Raczynski, D., and C. Serrano. 1988. ¿Planificación para el desarrollo local? La experiencia de algunos municipios de Santiago. *Colección Estudios CIEPLAN N° 24.*

——. eds. 1992. *Políticas sociales, mujeres y gobierno local.* Santiago de Chile: CIEPLAN.

Shah, A. 1991. *Perspectives on the Design of Intergovernmental Fiscal Relations.* Working Paper N° 726. Washington, D.C.: The World Bank.

Tomic, B., and R. González. 1983. *Municipio y Estado: dimensiones de una relación clave.* Monografías sobre Empleo N° 27. Santiago de Chile: PREALC.

The World Bank. 1988. *Informe sobre el desarrollo mundial 1988.* Washington, D.C.

———. 1992. *Chile: Subnational Government Finance.* Washington, D.C.

Comment

Sylvia Maxfield
Associate Professor, Yale University

Díaz-Alejandro's work had an interdisciplinary reach, in many ways as influential among students of political development as among students of economic development. It is especially fitting, therefore, that in this chapter Marcel suggests that decentralization is, in practice, a political process. My comments focus on the relationship between the economic and political aspects of decentralization.

Decentralization is especially appealing because it provides ways to make economic liberalization and democratization mutually reinforcing. The behemoth national state is able to retreat from what has been seen as nefarious economic intervention by delegating and devolving authority over economic and social policy to local governments. This makes for a happy marriage between political and economic liberalization in two ways. First, to the extent that local government is democratized, the provision of public goods and services by local administrators should yield significant efficiency gains. The theory is that public needs for government-provided goods and services are geographically diverse. Provision of these goods by local governments, which respond to local public preferences, eliminates misallocation of public resources.

As this chapter rightly points out, the economic efficiency gains from decentralization depend on the existence of mechanisms through which local residents can reveal their preferences for government-supplied goods and services and hold local government responsible for meeting these preferences. Local democratization is the best means for doing this. Mr. Marcel also notes that this could be accomplished through migration, which would be less felicitous for the marriage of political and economic liberalization.

Decentralization of political authority is also important to the happy marriage of political and economic liberalization in a second way. It adds to the chances of successful union to the extent that devolution or delegation of political authority can be made acceptable as compensation for the sometimes severe, short-term, and sector-specific economic losses resulting from liberalization. In essence, local democratization can be a powerful palliative for losses associated with a decline in national-level economic intervention and subsidy.

So what is local democracy? It is a lot more than elections, as Marcel rightly notes. He suggests that municipal democracy must entail both the widening of local electoral space and the creation of mechanisms for the public to express their preferences on an ongoing basis as the government makes policy choices and engages in policy implementation.

The first thing I want to emphasize is that in order for macroeconomic and macro-political liberalization to be mutually reinforcing there needs to be local democratization, understood as something that goes beyond conventional ideas of democracy. Increasingly, political scientists are stressing the Tocquevillian idea that democratic governance depends on the density of associational life in civil society.[1] Local democratization depends not only on the holding of elections but also on the state's acceptance of the right of citizens to pursue their goals autonomously. A wide range of political systems, including many that hold regular elections, oblige poor people to sacrifice their political rights in exchange for access to distributive programs. This is called clientelism, and it interferes with the exercise of citizenship rights. The problem is how subordinated people make the transition from clients to citizens. Citizenship entails nonconditional generalized political rights, while clientelism refers to the inherently selective and conditional distribution of resources and power based on ties of personal and political loyalty.

This transition from allocation of public services on the basis of patron-client relations to allocation on the basis of shared ideas of citizenship is what needs to occur at a local level for there to be the kind of democratization that makes for the felicitous marriage of efficient economic liberalization and democratic consolidation. Unfortunately, clientelism can be especially hard to break down in noncentral areas, which tend to be rural.

Violent regimes have been extraordinarily resilient in parts of the developing world. In Mexico, political entrepreneurs have replaced antiquated mechanisms for enforcing the exchange of political rights for social welfare with very sophisticated ones. Effective citizenship requires the ability and capacity to participate autonomously in politics and to take purposive action to shape government decisions and enforce government accountability. For the rural poor, attaining this often hinges on the balance of power between autonomous social movements, authoritarian local elites reluctant to cede power, national party cadres, and reformist state managers defined as those willing to accept increased associational autonomy. The transition from client to citizen comes through a long recursive cycle of bargaining between these actors.

---

[1] See Jonathan Fox, The Difficult Transition from Clientelism to Citizenship: Lessons from Mexico, *World Politics* 46 (January 1994):2, from which the following comments draw heavily.

Because this is a process that can take time, we cannot expect decentralization to be a panacea.

Evaluating the prospects for success of the decentralization-cum-local-democratization process in any given country can be difficult because it requires local-level knowledge of autonomous social movements and their relationship with local elites. Nevertheless attention to the national political environment is also telling. As Marcel points out, the Pinochet government was an obstacle to the kind of local democratization necessary to insure the efficiency of decentralization because decentralization did not involve increasing the possibilities for direct democracy at the local level. In the current macropolitical environment there is greater opportunity for genuine local democratization. The role of the national political environment in fostering conditions for local democratization is also evident in Mexico, a case I know better than the Chilean one. It appears that the PRI's electoral fortunes depend to a large extent on maintaining cliental relationships in rural Mexico that guarantee it votes in exchange for limited social goods. The PRI can democratize elections in urban Mexico and still win a plurality if it maintains control of the countryside. This macropolitical logic presents an important obstacle to the transition from clientelism to citizenship in rural municipalities in Mexico.

There is a generalizable rule here about the way the macropolitical environment is likely to affect local democratization. It echoes one of the conclusions Ranis and Stewart come to in their work on decentralization.[2] They conclude that the transition from clientelism to citizenship is likely to be most difficult in situations in which the state plays a dominant role in structuring the system of interest representation. This is most likely to occur where there are single or dominant party systems. Building support for parties that could challenge these one-party or dominant-party systems from those in rural or noncentral areas is made difficult by limited access to information and the way violence and bribery can limit the extent to which mass-based social and economic protests translate into party identifications and issue-based voting behavior. For autonomous social organizations, the most successful route to local democratization will combine efforts to work with national parties and efforts to fortify representative and autonomous economic interest groups.

Given that the regional level is often crucial in real world cases of incipient decentralization, another problem in realizing the benefits of

---

[2] Gustav Ranis and Frances Stewart, Government Decentralization and Participation. Paper prepared for the Human Development Report 1993 of United Nations Development Programme (UNDP).

decentralization is that the decentralized poor need to be able to engage in democratic collective action at the regional as well as the local level. For example, as Marcel points out, the widening of the decentralization effort in Chile in 1992 involved giving increased responsibility to regional governments over the allocation of public investment resources. Regional democratic collective action, however, is hampered by the dispersion of communities and the diversity of economic activities even within single regions.

The first point I have stressed in response to Marcel's paper is that the successful marriage of macroeconomic and political liberalization that can come from decentralization rests on local democratization understood in nontraditional ways. The second point I want to emphasize briefly, in conclusion, is that this marriage may also rest on the existence of a national strategy to cope with massive local dislocations that can come from economic liberalization and decentralization. In the best of cases the kinds of compensatory programs developed at a national level to cope with the dislocations caused by economic liberalization have reinforced trends toward local democratization. So-called "demand-based" antipoverty funds targeted to meet the challenge of making structural economic adjustment politically viable are being experimented with by a wide variety of countries. Bolivia's Emergency Social Fund, for example, allocated resources in response to proposals from local and municipal governments. Chilean antipoverty funds have also been allocated in a way that strengthens local citizenship. Some also contend that Mexico's Pronasol program has, in some instances, helped erode clientelism in both central and noncentral areas. In El Salvador and Peru antipoverty programs designed to compensate for dislocations caused by liberalization have reinforced the existing client and semi-cliental allocation of public goods in noncentral areas.

By way of conclusion let me say that the Chilean case, as described by Marcel, highlights what is necessary for decentralization to be the underpinning of a happy union between political and economic liberalization: first, local democratization that extends beyond traditional election-based conceptions of democracy to the building of citizenship in place of clientalism; and, second, the establishment of national compensatory antipoverty funds administered in such as way as to reinforce the replacement of clientelism with citizenship.

CHAPTER

4

Wretched Statecraft: Brazil's Vicious Circle

Rogério L.F. Werneck[1]

As has happened in most of the world, views on the economic role of the state have changed dramatically in Latin America during the last two decades. By the early seventies, most of the best trained economists in the region had developed a strong belief in the benefits of a wide range of direct government interventions in many areas of the economy. Keynesian triumphalism, then already fading in the United States and Europe, still thrived in Latin America, where Iberian tradition and a long historical experience of government intervention provided especially fertile soil for the idea of giving the state an important strategic economic role. Impressionistic arguments in favor of government intervention in the allocation of resources were then being replaced in the region by more rigorous ones, under the also late-coming influence of applied welfare economics and its "anatomy of market failures."[2]

Two decades later a totally different view on the economic role of the state has emerged in Latin America in the wake of a mountain of difficulties imposed by two oil shocks, a long foreign debt crisis, deep fiscal imbalance, prolonged stagnation, and high inflation. Those difficulties, as well as the market-oriented policies that helped some countries in the region to emerge successfully from the crisis, have amplified in Latin America the recent worldwide fall-of-the-Berlin-Wall effect on the dominant view about the desirable economic role of the state.

---

[1] The author is grateful to Dionísio D. Carneiro, Marcelo de P. Abreu, and Daniel R. de Oliveira for helpful comments and to Mônica Baumgarten for research assistance.
[2] See Bator (1958).

As the pendulum swings to an extreme market-oriented approach to policy making, overshooting becomes unavoidable as some countries in the region seem to be engaged in a kind of contest to establish the fastest reduction in the economic role of the state. A more balanced view is bound to emerge in the coming years as the difficult choice between market failures and government failures is reconsidered more pragmatically.[3]

This paper deals with some issues that should be taken into account in relation to that choice. Most of them are related to the appalling situation of the state apparatus in some countries—deeply affected by a very long crisis—and to how this is likely to constrain the policy choices of these countries in the future. The analysis basically refers to Brazil, but some arguments also fit other countries in the region.

Some Latin American economies have overcome the recent crisis and are apparently en route to growth and modernization. That is, however, not the case with Brazil. Quite the contrary, the Brazilian economy—and that means roughly 45 percent of Latin America and the Caribbean—is still struggling with unsolved mega-inflation and stagnation problems. Since the early eighties, recurrent stabilization attempts have not only consistently failed but have also, in general, amplified the difficulties to be faced. Present political obstacles make it hard to believe that successful stabilization will be attained before 1995.

From 1980 to 1982, the annual inflation rate in Brazil was already over 90 percent. It jumped to more than 200 percent from 1983 to 1985 and, after falling to 65 percent in 1986 in the wake of the Cruzado Plan, reached more than 400 percent in 1987. Inflation has been above 1,000 percent yearly since 1988, except in 1991, when it went down to 480 percent. Twelve years of unsuccessful stabilization attempts and half-hearted fiscal adjustment efforts have eroded the state's ability to formulate and implement economic policy, enlarging the scope for further failures in the future, in a vicious circle that has proved difficult to break so far. Analyzing the logic of this perverse process and the lessons that may be drawn from it is the main purpose of this chapter.

Government Failure and Statecraft

As is well known, the possibility of market failure has been the main rationale for government intervention in the economy. Awareness of situations in which market outcomes are inadequate has led to the prescription of corrective policies to deal with coordination failures of the price system.

---

[3] See Hirschman's (1982) insightful discussion on that choice.

Such situations may involve public goods, externalities, increasing returns to scale, incomplete information, imperfect competition, cyclical fluctuations in output and employment, and distributional inequity. The catalogue of market failures in economic theory has been seen for a long time as a guide for policy analysis and government intervention.[4] Yet there has also been a growing concern with government failures. It has been perceived that, in attempting to correct market failures, government may generate economic distortions that can be even more serious than those that inspired the policy actions. This called for a more balanced view on potential failures. As neatly put by Wolf (1979, p. 132):

> The existing theory of market failure provides a useful corrective to the theory of perfectly functioning markets. In a similar sense, the theory of nonmarket failure . . . is intended as a corrective for the implicit theory of perfectly functioning governments. Just as market failures or inadequacies have provided the theoretical underpinning for applied *policy analysis*, so nonmarket failures may provide the theoretical underpinning for *implementation analysis*. This is the analysis of how specific nonmarket activities (public policies) can be expected to operate and to depart in predictable ways from their costs and consequences as originally estimated.

In the conventional analysis of government failures, at least four sources of failure are identified.[5] First, the full consequences of many government actions are hard to trace in advance; second, government usually has only limited control over those consequences; third, policy designers do not have full control over policy implementation; and, fourth, there are agency problems (i.e., elected officials and public servants may have incentives to pursue objectives that are not in the public interest).

Of course, there is a large scope of government failures even when economic policy may rely on a good state apparatus. But this scope is certainly bound to be much larger when the state apparatus is somehow crippled, as seems to be the case in some Latin American countries. This point becomes even clearer when each of the four sources of failure mentioned above is considered separately. The worse the state apparatus, (1) the higher the probability of government not taking into account impor-

---

[4] See, for example, Inman (1987).
[5] See Stiglitz (1986) and Wolf (1979).

tant consequences of its possible actions when policy analysis and choice are being made; (2) the lower the degree of government control over unforeseen policy consequences; (3) the lower the degree of control policy designers have over policy implementation; and (4) the larger the scope for agency problems.

Since the importance of government failures is thus seen to be highly dependent on the condition of the state apparatus, it may be useful at this point to appeal to the notion of statecraft, an old Northern European word for the art of conducting state affairs. This word suggests that the practice of government is an art that demands skill, technique, and judgment, implying that government may be practiced well or poorly.[6] Competent economic policy and the capacity to keep government failures under control are an important part of good statecraft. Accordingly, poor statecraft may have disastrous economic consequences.

It is impossible to understand the deep economic crisis that affected much of Latin America in the eighties, and which is still affecting Brazil, without ascribing many of the difficulties to wretched statecraft. Moreover, in the Brazilian case, at least, there seems to be a vicious circle at work in which government failures generated by bad statecraft lead to a deterioration of the economic situation, which in turn feeds back into even worse statecraft. In the following sections some aspects of this cycle are examined.

Taking Stock: The Extent of the Macroeconomic Failure

From 1940 to 1980, Brazil sustained an average annual growth rate above 7 percent. This excellent performance was achieved despite the often serious political difficulties that were faced by the country during those four decades. Expansion was not only fast, but remarkably steady. In only six of the 40 years was the growth rate below 4 percent: 1942, 1947, 1956, and 1963–65; and in only one year, 1942, was there a fall in aggregate output. Real GDP increased by a factor of 15 in 40 years, meaning a five-fold increase in per capita output, since population had practically trebled in the same period. In 1990 dollars, per capita income grew from $600 to $3,000 during those four decades.

---

[6] See Anderson (1977, p. vii) and the Oxford English Dictionary. Notice that lately the term has often been used in a much narrower sense, as in Baldwin (1985, p. 9), to designate "the selection of means for the pursuit of foreign policy goals." However, in this paper the word statecraft is being used in its original, broader meaning.

These facts allow a proper perspective on the extent and consequences of the economic slowdown in the eighties and early nineties that resulted largely from government failure to deal with macroeconomic stabilization. In the 1981–92 period, the average annual growth rate of GDP was reduced to only 1.2 percent. In five of these 12 years there was a fall in real GDP. As the average population growth rate was slightly above 1.9 percent during the period, per capita GDP in 1992 was only $2,800, approximately 7 percent below its 1980 level.

Had the historical trend of the previous 40 years prevailed through the eighties and early nineties, the value of the Brazilian GDP in 1995 would reach approximately $1 trillion—roughly the present size of the British economy— instead of perhaps $440 billion, the probable value of GDP in 1995 if real output expansion equals population growth in the 1992–95 period. The corresponding level of per capita GDP—$6,300 instead of the $2,800 that will probably be observed in 1995— would be equivalent to those of the poorest countries of the European Community today.[7]

Of course, one cannot argue that fast growth could have been sustained despite all the difficulties faced by the Brazilian economy in the early eighties, particularly the external ones. From a long-term perspective, however, this period may be seen as a costly interruption in the growth trajectory of the Brazilian economy. The above counter-factual exercise provides at least an upper-range benchmark for the magnitudes involved in terms of the cost of that interruption, which to a large extent has to be attributed to the cycle connecting wretched statecraft and government failure to design and implement an effective macroeconomic stabilization policy. For a poor country that has not yet been able to provide for its inhabitants' most elementary needs in food, health, education and housing, the social dimensions of that cost are even more dramatic than the idea of wealth foregone.

"Something Has to Be Done" and "They Will Probably Do It Again"

Before trying to look into the roots of this vicious circle that is pushing failure deep into the nineties, it may be useful to try to understand how this perverse process has recently been affecting the formulation and implementation of macroeconomic policy in the country. As expected, the very critical situation of the Brazilian economy brings about from

---

[7] This counter-factual exercise updates a similar one made in Werneck (1988).

time to time a widespread feeling that "something has to be done," which means that government is increasingly pressed to act.[8] Under such conditions, poor statecraft may lead to really disastrous results. Badly designed, often grandiose measures have proved to be the most probable outcome, as the government tacitly or even openly accepted the Napoleonic dictum—*"On s'engage et puis on voit"*—to justify improvised and grossly inconsistent policy packages.[9] Indeed, in trying to be credible, policy makers have often made the decision to "burn the ships" *à la* Cortez.

This process has been exacerbated by the present Brazilian economic debate. As often happens to countries affected by a very deep and long economic crisis—some Eastern European countries, at the moment, seem to constitute comparable cases—Brazil has become an open market for ideas, both locally developed and imported, about how to overcome the crisis. Most of these ideas are simple nonsense, but again poor statecraft leaves the government and, therefore, the country relatively unprotected against them. All sorts of proposals, ranging from another general price freeze to varied forms of default on the domestic public debt, or even to resuming economic growth as a way to fight a 30 percent monthly inflation, are popping up daily in the press. One even finds finance ministers publicly confessing that they are trying to assemble a new stabilization package combining parts taken from this box of nonsensical proposals.

As policies fail, one after another, the economy has to cope with the accumulated long-lasting negative effects of those failures, which tend to render future policy making even more complex. Expectations generated by the permanent possibility that government may suddenly announce a new policy package, representing another major discontinuity in the steering of economic policy, have amplified the difficulties of implementing a successful stabilization plan. As the effects of the last unsuccessful package fade away, the public starts to fear that "they (the government) will probably do it again." In the late eighties those expectations mainly led to widespread preemptive price hikes, when it was

---

[8] An example may be enlightening at this point. On his 43rd day as Finance Minister, the third in six months of the Itamar Franco administration, Eliseu Resende was getting the following piece of advice from the press, by means of an influential column: "To exorcise the specter of immobilization, the president has no other way out but to adopt a clear-cut economic policy. Orthodox or heterodox . . . leftist or rightist. The tag does not matter, or whether it is a gradual policy or the announcement of a new package. The only thing that matters is action." (*Jornal do Brasil,* April 13, 1993.)

[9] This dictum is well remembered by Wolf (1979) in his discussion of policy implementation.

believed that a new price freeze might be announced. As the result was an even faster acceleration of inflation, that often contributed to precipitating the announcement of a freeze.[10]

Lately, however, after a large part of the economy's financial assets had been blocked for 18 months in the Central Bank by the Collor I Plan, expectations have diminished even more. Though the assets were returned to their holders as promised, the fear that some variant of such a measure may be announced again has led to permanent worries about economic agents making sudden preemptive moves in their portfolio decisions, increasing their demand for foreign currency and real assets. Again, that has rendered macroeconomic management even more difficult.[11]

Long-lasting negative effects may also stem from badly prepared and implemented reforms, also induced by the feeling that "something has to be done." The claim for making sweeping and profound economic reforms has led government to try to carry out some of those reforms piecemeal; but, again, poor statecraft has often led to badly designed reforms, which have jeopardized the original public support for them. Such experiences show that, though government is often not competent enough to conduct reforms as required, in general it is sufficiently empowered to try. And the results may be so bad as to lead to an arrangement that is even worse than the pre-reform situation and much more difficult to change, given the naturally strong opposition that the announcement of still another reform would generate. The best example of such fiascos is probably the so-called Santana public service reform of 1990–91, which greatly reinforced the deterioration of statecraft in Brazil, as will be seen in the next section.[12]

The Bureaucratic Elite and the Quality of the Economic Policy

It is certainly true that the existence of a capable bureaucratic elite does not constitute a sufficient condition for good statecraft. But it is also true that without a reasonably good bureaucratic elite, poor statecraft becomes a much more probable outcome. Since the mid-eighties, there

---

[10] See Modiano (1990) for an analysis of the recurrent stabilization shocks of the late eighties.

[11] There is another long-lasting effect that should be mentioned. Though capital flight used to be relatively unimportant in Brazil during the eighties (compared for instance to Mexico, Argentina, and Venezuela), defensive behavior in portfolio management after the traumatic experience of the Collor I Plan in 1990 has increased the importance of Brazilian residents' assets held abroad.

[12] After João Santana, the first public administration secretary of the Collor administration.

Table 4.1. Brazil: Federal Government Payroll, 1990–92

Year	Value as percentage of GDP	Index Number Value as Percentage of GDP 1990 = 100
1990	4.30	100.0
1991	3.53	82.1
1992	3.32	77.2

Source: Departamento do Tesouro Nacional.

has been a systematic decay in the quality of the highest echelons of the federal bureaucracy in Brazil. This constitutes a complex process resulting from the interaction of many determinants. It may be useful, however, to single out some of them and to show that government failures have played an important role in that process and, therefore, to pinpoint one of the important elements of the vicious circle linking government failures and poor statecraft.

A first link was the perverse effect of the cutback in the value of the federal government's payroll as part of recurrent, though half-hearted, fiscal adjustment efforts, with severe reductions in the salary level of the bureaucratic elite, particularly since 1990. From 1990 to 1992, the value of the federal government's annual payroll was reduced from 4.3 percent to 3.32 percent of the GDP, a 22.8 percent reduction in two years, as shown in Table 4.1. Unable to dismiss public employees, the government resorted to reducing their salaries. Nominal salaries of top public servants were consistently readjusted well below inflation during this period; in the Ministry of Planning, for instance, the monthly top real salary level for economists during most of 1992 was only approximately 20 percent of what it used to be in either March 1985 or March 1988. Table 4.1 illustrates the continuing decline of their real salary levels at the beginning of this decade.[13]

Immediately after taking office in March 1990, President Collor announced a major public administration reform that would lead to either the dismissal or the retirement of hundreds of thousands of federal public servants, drastically reduce the number of government cars, and encourage the sale of government housing facilities that were being rented out at nominal fees to high-ranking bureaucrats in Brasília. When

---

[13] Deflated by IGP-DI, the general price index. The author is grateful to Ricardo Varsano from IPEA for supplying the salary data.

announced, that reform proved to be resoundingly popular. It also introduced the so-called *regime único* (one rule), which meant that the contracts of all public employees would have to be submitted to the same set of specific rules, different from those that regulate work contracts in the private sector. This imposed a change in the work contracts of a large number of public servants who had been hired under rules that applied to the private sector.

As already mentioned, the reform ended up as a total fiasco. A provision of the 1988 Constitution establishes that after five years in public service a public employee may be fired only when accused of very serious misbehavior; this left most of the federal bureaucracy sheltered from the government's dismissal plans. Approximately 50,000 public servants were in fact dismissed, relatively few compared to the almost 1 million paychecks on the federal government's payroll. Furthermore, under the new *regime único*, it became much more difficult, both politically and legally, to protect the salary levels of the bureaucratic elite, a large part of whom used to be hired by public foundations and other autonomous public agencies, which had their own salary policies. Incentives for early retirement, when coupled with the drastic reduction in real salaries in 1990, led to the retirement of a large part of the most-talented high-level public servants.[14]

Recruiting new high-ranking public officers has become extremely difficult, as new ministers have rapidly found. Not only have salaries become very unattractive, but housing costs in Brasília for new staff went up dramatically as 11,000 government apartments were sold at a small fraction of their market value to public servants lucky enough to be occupying them during the 1990–91 period. Admittedly, people are often attracted to work for the government with other benefits in mind, such as, for example, the power to influence decisions or the possibility of a political career. Therefore, the above-mentioned difficulties in recruiting new, high-level public servants could perhaps have been bypassed had they not been amplified by the extremely high ministerial turnover, particularly in the ministries responsible for the steering of economic policy.

---

[14] As a result of mass retirement, some strategic functions of the federal government apparatus, such as tax collection, were gravely affected. Undermanning has become a major problem in *Receita Federal* (the tax collection agency), which has been forced to function with fewer than 5,000 tax officers nationwide, half of them allocated to customs clearance and bureaucratic tasks. Training new tax officers takes at least four years. On the early retirement of some of the most competent tax officers, see "Longe do Poder, mas Perto do Dinheiro," *Exame*, April 14, 1993.

Figure 4.1. Top Monthly Real Salary Level for Planning Ministry Economists, January 1990-March 1993
(Top Monthly Real Salary in March 1985 = 100)

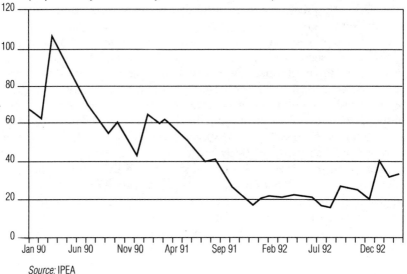

Source: IPEA

As seen in Table 4.2, from March 1985, when the military regime reached its end, to May 1993, Brazil had nine different finance ministers, not including the present one. On the average, each of them lasted approximately 11 months. The average is a little higher for the Sarney and Collor administrations: 15 months in both cases; but it has been reduced to only 2.5 months in the current Franco administration, at least up to this point.[15]

---

[15] Even though a historical benchmark is difficult to establish, 2.5 months is certainly a very low average. From 1946 to 1954, during the Dutra and (second) Vargas administrations, this average was 20.6 months. It went down to 5.7 months during the unstable period that followed the Vargas suicide and up again to 20 months during the Kubitschek administration (1956–61), falling to 6.3 months in the also unstable period of the Quadros and Goulart administrations (1961–64). During the military period (1964–85), each finance minister lasted an average of 50.4 months. See Abreu (1990).

Table 4.2. Brazilian Finance Ministers, March 1985–March 1993

Administration and ministers	Period	Number of months as minister	Average number of months of incumbency
Sarney administration	**March 85–March 90**		15.0
Francisco Dornelles	March 85–Sept. 85	6	
Dilson Funaro	Sept. 85–June 87	20	
Luiz Carlos Bresser Pereira	May 87–Dec. 87	7	
Maílson da Nóbrega	Dec. 87–March 90	27	
Collor administration	**March 90–Sept. 92**		15.0
Zélia Cardoso de Mello [a]	March 90–May 91	14	
Marcílio Marques Moreira [a]	May 91–Sept. 92	16	
Franco administration	**Oct. 92–present**		2.5[b]
Gustavo Krause	Oct. 92–Dec. 92	3	
Paulo Haddad	Dec. 92–Feb. 93	2	
Eliseu Resende	March 93–May 93	2	
Fernando Henrique Cardoso	May 93–present	–	
Overall average number of months of incumbency			10.9[b]

Notes:
[a] Minister of Economy, as the Collor administration eliminated the Ministry of Finance, which was later recreated by the Franco Administration.
[b] Does not include Fernando Henrique Cardoso, the current minister.

Another link in the cycle connecting government failures and poor statecraft is therefore established. As ministers tumble one after another in the wake of unsuccessful stabilization programs, both the new minister and the people whom he tries to attract to work with him know that he will not last long, probably a few months. Assembling a competent economic team under such conditions becomes exceedingly difficult. Added to this is the fact that the mediocre team that he will finally be able to form will only make his fate more hopeless from the outset. In fact, this has made even the recruitment of ministers and Central Bank chairmen increasingly difficult, as many talented candidates have lately refused invitations from the president. With a brand new economic team in charge of policy formulation and implementation every few months, it is not surprising that results have been, to say the least, so disappointing. Moreover, the high turnover of economic teams has made the federal government much more exposed to the effects of widespread rent-seeking and outright corruption by important segments of Brazilian society.

Political Constraints on the Quality of Economic Policy:
Democratization, Congress, Federalism, and the Constitution

The roots of poor statecraft since the mid-eighties can be found in the difficulties faced during the redemocratization period after the end of the military regime in early 1985. Unluckily, Tancredo Neves, an able and influential politician who had been elected the first president of the civilian regime by an impressive coalition of political forces, died before taking office, opening the way to a considerably less talented and less influential vice-president. During the first three years of Sarney's administration, Congress drafted a new constitution that was finally promulgated in late 1988. Unfortunately, the long and delicate political negotiations that led to that constitution took place exactly when the central government was particularly feeble due to the shortcomings of President Sarney, who was accidentally inducted into office and continuously motivated by the quest for a higher degree of legitimacy.

In fact, the central government became even more feeble after the failure of two stabilization shocks, in 1986 and 1987. In another link in the chain, the room for even poorer statecraft was substantially enlarged through a major constitutional reform blunder in 1988. Because the complex coalition of political forces that had been assembled behind Tancredo Neves could not be maintained, a newly formed coalition in Congress, which was strongly influenced by state and local governments, managed to approve a new constitution that redesigned the previous fiscal-federalism arrangement and diminished the fiscal powers of the Union Government, while greatly enlarging the federal government's expenditure obligations. It was not only an inconsistent fiscal federalism arrangement that was being established but, as Bacha and Lamounier (1992, p. 23) put it so well, "the abstractly desirable goal of decentralization prevailed over any consideration of timing, further weakening the central government at a moment when the Brazilian inflationary monster seemed again untamable."

These changes in the fiscal-federalism arrangement deserve closer attention.[16] As is well known, the Brazilian state is a particularly complex and multifarious entity that unfolds at three different government levels: the central government, more than two dozen state governments, and approximately 5,000 local governments. Each has both executive and legislative branches. The legal framework that regulates intergovernmental relations within this intricate system was shown to have many

---

[16] For a fuller discussion of fiscal federalism in Brazil, see Affonso (1992).

deficiencies, especially after the 1988 Constitution was adapted, in which, as just noted, the interests that should have been defended by the central government were not properly taken into consideration.

When the Constitution was promulgated, it was greeted by many analysts as an important move toward the decentralization of power in the country, since it reduced the central government's importance. However, since 1988 the deficiencies of the new fiscal federalism arrangement have become increasingly clear. The central government has lost a substantial part of its tax revenue to states and local governments, without being able to transfer to them any significant part of its spending programs. Nevertheless, as the new fiscal system is being phased in, states and local governments are not only quickly adjusting their spending in response to their fast-growing revenue, but are spending well above their recently enlarged means.

The present fiscal federalism arrangement is clearly imposing severe difficulties on stabilization policy in Brazil. What happened in 1990 well illustrates the difficulties involved. The central government's fiscal austerity efforts were partly offset by state and local governments overspending in the wake of an electoral campaign. This also had a serious impact on the steering of monetary policy, since part of the higher borrowing requirements of state and local governments were financed by state banks, which ended up being bailed out by the Central Bank under the political pressure of governors with good access to the presidency.

Facing the need to accept a long-term fiscal adjustment, the central government has been severely constrained by the obligation to transfer to lower levels a large proportion of the revenue from personal income, profit, and excise taxes on industrialized products, knowing in advance that any transfer will be immediately spent by state and local governments. This drain seriously reduces the effectiveness of the overall fiscal effort and thus the possibilities of stabilization policy.[17] This, in turn, has led to a search for exotic federal taxes, capable of generating resources not shared with state and local governments, which has meant a further deterioration of the quality of the tax system.

Most state governments in Brazil have become clearly over-indebted. And the federal government has been pressed hard by state governors to "solve" their debt problems. Facing the possibility of rejection by Congress of the fiscal adjustment package submitted in late 1991, the federal government finally agreed to include in the package an

---

[17] See Werneck (1992) for a fuller analysis of the present difficulties imposed by fiscal federalism on stabilization policy in Brazil.

ample rescheduling of the states' debts. The part of the debt owed either to the federal government or to any of its financial institutions would be rescheduled to be paid over 20 years. The state bonds held by the private investors, which pay a very high interest rate, would be exchanged for lower-cost federal bonds.

This new legislation only established the guidelines that bilateral rescheduling agreements between each state and the federal government should follow. To avoid the inducement for a large future increase in the states' deficits (the moral hazard problem) the federal government succeeded in including in the debt-rescheduling legislation a restraint on the states' new debt issues. To be able to reschedule its debt, a state would be required to agree not to issue any new debt for a number of years, the penalty for failing to obey that clause being simply to render the rescheduling agreement null and void.

Before any agreement had been signed, the largest states were manifesting their resistance to that clause and considered the possibility of forcing Congress to approve required changes in the legislation. Negotiations that should have led to compromise agreements were suspended during the political crisis that ended with the impeachment of President Collor. A new debt rescheduling law was approved by Congress in late 1992, but states are still resisting the acceptance of any limits on their power to issue new debt—even the narrow restraint the new rescheduling law imposes on debt issued in the form of state treasury bills. Without the imposition of such limits, debt rescheduling will turn out to have been just another policy blunder that will simply reestablish the states' ability to become overindebted again in the future, maintaining their soft budget constraint and, therefore, a major source of macroeconomic disequilibrium.[18]

Besides introducing an inconsistent fiscal federalism arrangement that amplified the Union's burden in the required fiscal adjustment effort, the new constitution did not contribute to the task of endowing the state that was emerging from the long military period with "a coherent . . . machinery against the multiple pressures of an emerging mass democracy, of a huge electorate (and) of a new generation of independent and aggressive labor leaders."[19] In fact, it amplified the scope for the widespread rent-seeking behavior of many segments of the Brazilian society, imposing upon the federal budget a considerable additional bur-

---

[18] See Werneck (1992).
[19] Bacha and Lamounier (1992, p. 26).

den, exactly when the Union's fiscal resources were being reduced in favor of state and local governments.[20]

Building up a New State: The Quest for Better Statecraft

There is a widespread view in Brazil today that the key to overcoming the economic crisis that the country has been facing for more than a decade is fundamental public sector reform, so fundamental that it would perhaps be more appropriate to say that what is needed is to reconstruct the public sector from its present ruins. Reconstructing the public sector constitutes a challenge that will probably take many years to be properly addressed.

Both in Brazil and abroad, there are many who believe that what is happening in the country is the failure and bankruptcy of the state, in flagrant contrast to the vigor of the private sector and the liveliness of civil society. According to this view, a fundamentally healthy society is being precluded from exploiting its ample possibilities by a sick state. As all evils are thus ascribed to the state, what should be done is to excise them so as to pull the state up to the level of Brazilian society.

Unhappily, that is a distorted view, even though it sounds attractive, simple, relatively optimistic, and easy to exploit for political reasons. What is happening in Brazil is much more than the failure of the state. The present state is largely an endogenous outcome of Brazilian society. The crisis is therefore much deeper and much more comprehensive. It reflects the failure of a society in dealing with the basic political problem of organizing and maintaining a state capable of acting according to the fundamental interests of that society.

The state in Brazil continues to be what it is and to serve the interests of the majority of the Brazilian society poorly simply because that society has not yet found proper forms of political organization to make a better state feasible. That means that the problem is a much more serious one. It is not simply a crisis that can be laid at the doorstep of the state. It involves society as a whole and poses a serious challenge to its elite.

Discouragement in the face of that challenge has increased the seductive power of the idea that the state is practically dispensable. Of course, that is nothing but a mirage. Looking at modern societies, one may see that there is ample room for choice. There are cases in which the

---

[20] On the perverse effects of rent-seeking behavior on macroeconomic performance, see Olson (1982).

state has assumed great importance and other cases in which it plays a much more limited role. In many societies the state has acquired excessive proportions, and most of these are now painfully trying to cut it down to manageable size. There is, however, no case of a country that has managed without a modern state, endowed with a fairly competent and scrupulous bureaucracy and able to act at acceptable levels of efficiency in areas that will always be reserved for the state. Modernization and development are not feasible without constructing a modern state, no matter how economically and politically liberal the development path is. That is the hard reality that Brazilian society has to face today.[21]

Reconstructing the public sector will require many constitutional amendments. In early October 1993, Congress started to discuss what could become a major reform of the Constitution, following a clause that opens up the possibility of having amendments approved by a 50 percent majority for a limited period, five years after the new Constitution has been promulgated. Such reconstruction involves, first of all, a tax reform that broadens the tax base, reduces tax rates, and modernizes the tax collecting apparatus. It also involves rebuilding the public service, correcting the blunder of the disastrous administrative reform of 1990–91, and eliminating the rigidities and wrong incentives imposed by the impossibility of dismissing public servants. The reconstruction of the public sector also demands a new fiscal federalism arrangement, in which the distribution of fiscal resources among the three levels of government is consistent with the distribution of expenditure functions among them.

Imposing fiscal responsibility on state and local governments is one of the most urgently required measures. That means granting the Central Bank sufficient political autonomy to assure that public-owned financial institutions—federal ones included—are managed in a way that is not detrimental to macroeconomic stability. Reconstructing the social security system and restoring the public-sector savings generation capability—in order to resume government social investment programs—constitute other required measures.

It certainly is a very heavy reform agenda that will probably take years to be properly implemented. Brazil's vicious circle, however, will not be broken before a wide enough political coalition can assure the joint implementation of a reasonably large portion of these reforms.

---

[21] Part of the difficulties that have to be faced in the task of constructing a modern state may be ascribed to the fact that "competent government" is actually a public good that therefore tends to be undersupplied. See Stiglitz (1986).

Much attention is given today in Brazil to the idea of redesigning the political representation itself, the "network of relationships and procedures that formally determines who authorizes whom to do what, and under what conditions."[22] The reintroduction of a parliamentary system was rejected by the electorate in a plebiscite held in late April 1992.[23]

A sizeable segment of the Congress is, however, becoming more sensitive to the idea of overhauling the electoral legislation in order to strengthen political parties and improve the quality of political representation. What is envisaged is the emergence of a stable majority coalition that may finally lead to a higher degree of commitment by the Congress with respect to the steady steering of economic policy. Such an outcome would certainly make room for a much improved level of statecraft. In addition, the general elections to be held in late 1994, in which both a new congress and a new president will be simultaneously elected, may provide a unique opportunity for a more collaborative relationship between the executive and legislative branches in the second half of the nineties.

---

[22] Bacha and Lamounier (1992), p. 26.

[23] There was a short-lived parliamentary experience in the country after the Quadros resignation, which lasted from September 1961 to January 1963.

References

Abreu, M. de P. 1990. *A Ordem do Progresso: Cem Anos de Política Econômica Republicana.* Rio de Janeiro: Editora Campus.

Affonso, J.R. 1992. Federalismo Fiscal e Reforma Institucional: Falácias, Conquistas e Descentralização. Brasília. Mimeo.

Anderson, C.W. 1977. *Statecraft: An Introduction to Political Choice and Judgment.* New York: John Wiley.

Auerbach, A.J., and M. Feldstein, eds. 1987. *Handbook of Public Economics.* Amsterdam: North-Holland.

Bacha, E., and B. Lamounier. 1992. Redemocratization and the Impasse of Economic Reform in Brazil. Paper presented at the Overseas Development Council Workshop in Rio de Janeiro.

Baldwin, D.A., 1985. *Economic Statecraft.* Princeton: Princeton University Press.

Bator, F. 1958. Anatomy of Market Failure. *Quarterly Journal of Economics* 72:351–79.

Hirschman, A. 1982. *Shifting Involvements: Private Interest and Public Action.* Princeton: Princeton University Press.

Inman, R.P. 1987. *Markets, Governments and the "New" Political Economy.* In *Handbook of Public Economics, Vol. 2.* eds., A.J. Auerbach and M. Feldstein. Amsterdam: North-Holland.

Modiano, E. 1990. A Ópera dos Três Cruzados. In *A Ordem do Progresso: Cem Anos de Política Econômica Republicana.* ed. M. de P. Abreu. Rio de Janeiro: Editora Campus.

Olson, M. 1982. *The Rise and Decline of Nations: Economic Growth, Stagflation and Social Rigidities.* New Haven: Yale University Press.

Stiglitz, J. 1986, *Economics of the Public Sector.* New York: W.W. Norton.

Werneck, R.L.F. 1988. A Longa Transição dos Anos Oitenta. *Carta Econômica* (March).

———. 1992. *Fiscal Federalism and Stabilization Policy in Brazil.* Texto para Discussão n. 282. Departamento de Economia, PUC-Rio.

Wolf C. Jr., 1979. A Theory of Nonmarket Failure: Framework for Implementation Analysis. *The Journal of Law and Economics* 22(1):107–39.

Comment

Pedro S. Malan

This chapter is well written, thought-provoking, and clearly of interest to a much wider audience than just anguished Brazilians, a chapter that Carlos Díaz-Alejandro would have been delighted to read and comment upon. My own comments are organized in three parts: (1) the more general issues raised; (2) the specific, somber assessment of the current Brazilian situation; and (3) the implications of the analysis for those involved in, or concerned with, economic, social, and political change in other countries going through the painful processes of structural change.

Market Reforms Require an Effective State[1]

The paper could be seen as a contribution to the growing literature on "governance capacity" in developing countries. The author appropriately recovers an old Northern European word for it—statecraft—and links it with another growing concern about government failures: the recurring observation that, in attempting to correct well-known market failures, governments may generate further economic distortions that can be even more serious than the market failures that inspired the policy interventions in the first place.

The likelihood of such a perverse outcome is sharply increased by poor statecraft or low capacity for governance—that is, a relative lack of the state's capability to diagnose, formulate, and consistently implement macro- and microeconomic policies.

This may seem a bit trivial and tautological at first sight, but the author is bent on "analyzing the logic of this perverse process and the lessons that may be drawn from it"—and not only for Brazil. In doing so, the author goes well beyond the conventional and trivial assertion that "better policies lead to better results, worse policies to worse results," so often repeated without much analysis by too many policy advisers from certain multilateral institutions.

What, then, is new in Professor Werneck's general analysis? In my view, it is his attempt to explain the roots of the vicious circle whereby, as policies fail one after another, the economy has to cope with the accumulated, long-lasting, negative effects of those failures. All this tends to make current and future policy making even more complex and difficult,

---

[1] This is one of the fundamental points underlying M. Naim's (1993) excellent book.

adding to the so-called "credibility issues" that go along with the formulation and implementation of any set of policy actions.

Governments, no matter how weak, are always under pressure to act (the "something has to be done" syndrome) and, indeed, always retain some power to do these "somethings." At the same time, the rest of society rightly bets that, indeed, "the government will probably try again" and takes all sorts of defensive measures in the light of past, failed experiences. The list of defensive measures includes anticipatory price increases, tax evasion, capital flight, increased risk premiums on government bonds, and so forth. Such defensive measures obviously undermine the very attempts at policy changes—especially when undertaken by governments with "wretched statecraft capabilities," which (unfortunately) have been observed in far too many countries.

The fundamental point emerging from the analysis in this chapter is related to the quest for better governance capabilities, a quest that requires profound public sector reforms. This is definitely not equivalent to the oft-mentioned need simply to reduce the size of the state apparatus. In many cases, this is a worthy objective but is not in itself a solution. That solution usually involves the attempt to operate a leaner, to be sure, but also much more efficient and stronger state apparatus, at least in some crucial agencies and institutions.

All the recent emphasis on private sector development (which, in fact, should have been on enhancing the role and the contribution of the private sector to development) is meaningless if not accompanied by at least equal emphasis on rebuilding the state's capabilities as a *sine qua non* condition for a thriving and competitive private sector. One of the most unfortunate consequences of the often ideological debate of the 1980s was the presumption that the private and the public were opposite, antagonistic camps and that the retrenchment and weakening of the state would necessarily be to the private sector's benefit.[2]

Professor Werneck is surely right in expressing the hope that a more balanced view is bound to emerge in the coming years as the diffi-

---

[2] Rupert Pennant-Rea, for many years the editor of *The Economist* and currently deputy governor of the Bank of England, wrote the following in his farewell editorial: ". . . nor is it enough to have a philosophy that is probusiness, or even proenterprise, simply on the grounds that it is the private sector that delivers the goods. Rare is the businessman who, catching a whiff of subsidy in the air, does not start salivating. Every boardroom wants a tax break for its industry, every sales team longs for a market to itself. They may all shout for free enterprise, but they covet monopoly. This is not a criticism of them; it is, though, the axiom on which governments should build their policies, and journalists their contributions." *The Economist*, March 27, 1993, pp. 16–18.

cult choice between addressing market failures and government failures is more pragmatically reconsidered.

Brazil: Overcoming Skepticism

The paper provides a rather somber assessment of the current Brazilian situation, particularly the current state of Brazil's "governance capabilities." The reasons are well-known to a Brazilian or Latin American audience. Since March of 1985, when a 21-year period of military rule came to a soft end, Brazil has experienced six attempted stabilization programs. These have made only a brief dent in a continually growing rate of inflation, now one of the two or three most formidable in the world. Over that same period of time, Brazil has had 10 ministers of finance and 11 Central Bank presidents. It is obvious that consistent economic policies become exceedingly difficult to ensure under such conditions. The high turnover of economic teams has rendered the federal government much more exposed to the effects of widespread rent-seeking behavior by important segments of Brazilian society—not to mention outright corruption.

The severe reduction in salary levels of the country's bureaucratic elite, particularly since 1990, has sharply aggravated the effects of the high turnover rate at the top, since it has led to the mass retirement of talented, high-level, career civil servants, particularly from some strategic agencies of the federal government—such as the Internal Revenue Service, the Budget Office, and the National Treasury. Recruiting new high-ranking public officers has become extremely difficult, given the unattractiveness of the salaries and the uncertainties associated with instability. Professor Werneck rightly identifies this situation as another critical element in the cycle connecting government failures and poor statecraft.

Another ingredient of the "vicious circle," notes Professor Werneck, is the fact that the central government, which under the military was relatively strong (at least *vis-à-vis* the provincial states, the Congress, the judicial system, and corporatist interests), was made extremely weak by the 1988 Constitution *vis-à-vis* these four sets of political agents. The present fiscal federalism—the transfer of power from the federal government to states, Congress, the judiciary, and corporate interests—has clearly imposed severe difficulties on the implementation of consistent stabilization policies in Brazil by adding a considerable burden to the federal budget.

All this may seem more than enough to justify a relatively high degree of skepticism about Brazil's ability to overcome its current predicament. The legacies of the recent past seem a bit overwhelming when seen in the light of actual governance capabilities.

I believe, however, that Professor Werneck's assessment is far too skeptical and that, while all his points are well taken, on balance the country has been moving in the right direction, albeit in painfully slow motion. My reasons for a very guarded confidence in the future are largely related to today's growing recognition of precisely those critical aspects of the cycle that Professor Werneck has analyzed so well. There is growing support for addressing these factors, as well as a widely shared perception that inflation is the most inequitable tax imagineable for Brazil, since the more wealthy an individual is, the greater protection that individual is offered through daily-indexed financial instruments. There is a growing recognition that Brazil would slowly but inexorably move toward dollarization and eventual hyperinflation in the absence of determined and consistent programs to address the problem.

The most recent stabilization program, announced in December 1993, attempts to face squarely the financial and administrative disarray of the public sector. The government proposed a constitutional amendment that will ensure a zero operational balance in 1994 and in 1995 (thereby including the first year of the new administration scheduled to take charge on January 1, 1995). The government, moreover, proposed more than 70 amendments to the 1988 Constitution, most of which have to do with implementing the required change in the fiscal regime of the country. Finally, it clearly indicated the nature of the monetary reform it intends to implement after the fundamentals of the change in the fiscal regime are set in place by Congress, including the constitutional revision which should have been concluded by March 15, 1994.

In short, the current crisis—and the acceleration of inflation—are reinforcing the need to adopt the kind of policies put forth by the current administration in December 1993. Professor Werneck may be right in noting that the crisis also undercuts the viability of efforts to implement change. The jury is, however, still out—in fact, it will be out for some time because, as Professor Werneck rightly notes, "a very heavy reform agenda will probably take years to be properly implemented." He also rightly notes that "the Brazilian vicious circle will not be broken before a wide enough political coalition can assure the joint implementation of a reasonably large part of these reforms." This coalition is in the making, if for no other reason than because there is no alternative. A country such as Brazil cannot afford to drift aimlessly toward irrelevance and decay without a reaction from its political and economic elites.

The basic justification for this very guarded confidence is best expressed by a remarkable observation by Gramsci quoted in Naim (1993): "The ancient is dying and the new has yet to be born. In this interlude, monsters are bred." Brazil has bred its fair share of monsters in the recent past. Although we are still in the interlude, the relevant and increasingly shared agenda for reforms is not likely to include monsters. Countries, like people and institutions, I happen to believe, do learn from their mistakes and past experiences and tend to move pragmatically toward more sensible approaches as other possibilities are exhausted in the process.

The Main General Lessons

What are the main lessons or implications of the analysis contained in this chapter for those engaged in or committed to helping bring about stabilization, structural change, and social modernization in developing countries?

Underlying Professor Werneck's paper is the perception of the failing state as an endogenous outcome of society's failure to deal with the vital political issue of organizing and maintaining a system of general and stable rules, institutions that properly enforce them, and predictable mechanisms to settle conflicts over the rules and their enforcement. In other words, creating governance capability is a societal task that cannot be left to the public sector, since a competent government is actually a public good and therefore tends to be undersupplied.

In this connection, the essential point in Professor Werneck's analysis is worth quoting at length:

> Looking at modern societies, one may see that there is ample room for choice. There are cases in which the state has assumed great importance and other cases in which it plays a much more limited role. In many societies the state has acquired excessive proportions, and most of these are now painfully trying to cut it down to a manageable size. *There is, however, no case of a country that has managed without a modern state, endowed with a fairly competent and scrupulous bureaucracy and able to act at acceptable levels of efficiency in areas that will always be reserved for the state. Modernization and development are not feasible without constructing a modern state, no matter how economically and politically liberal the development path is* [emphasis added].

The author calls this "the hard reality that Brazilian society has to face today." In fact, this is the hard reality that most developing and former socialist countries have to face. Herein lies the general import of this chapter.

Policymakers in these countries, as well as the staff of international organizations, have always paid a lot of attention to the proper analysis (diagnosis) of a country's economic problems and to the formulation of policies designed to address such problems. It is clear by now that much more is at stake and that the critical problems are related to implementation capabilities, that is, governments' determination and commitment to pursue the proper objectives and to acquire credibility by building political coalitions in support of such policies. In democracies, this means building societal and parliamentary support.

These are not tasks that can be accomplished in societies with weak states, captured and numbed by all sorts of conflicting vested interests. Lest this last observation be misconstrued as supporting strong (in the sense of authoritarian) governments, let me conclude by expressing my strong view that an effectively functioning democracy is by far the best way to overcome such difficulties—even though the process may take a relatively longer period of time to be consolidated. In fact, it took some generations in today's industrial countries. It will not be that much different in the developing world, although the prevailing sense of urgency may help.

References

Naim, M. 1993. *Paper Tigers and Minotaurs: The Politics of Venezuela's Economic Reforms.* New York: The Carnegie Endowment.

Comment

José A. Scheinkman
Department of Economics
University of Chicago

Rogério Werneck has presented a thoughtful and provocative chapter trying to deal with the failure of Brazilian society to solve its economic crisis. This failure to design and implement adequate policies to deal with economic difficulties is a source of pain for Brazilians and of puzzlement for social scientists. Since many of the countries that have faced similar predicaments seem to have overcome their crisis, it is clear that part of Brazil's current problems must be attributed to "wretched statecraft." Werneck argues persuasively that the failures of economic management have in fact eroded the capacity of the state to formulate and carry on economic reforms, increasing the probability of future failures. His paper treats in detail two elements of this "vicious cycle": the decay of the quality of the federal bureaucracy and the new fiscal federalism of the 1988 Constitution.

The Quality of the Bureaucracy

In a society, talent must be allocated among the bureaucracy and alternative activities. A better bureaucrat is preferable to a worse one, but in many cases it is even more desirable to allocate the extra talent to the private sector or to the educational establishment. There is not much empirical evidence to help us reflect on the question of the optimal quality of bureaucrats. William Baumol (1990) argued that imperial China's impressively trained class of officials represented an overallocation of talent to the bureaucratic sector. Brazil's bureaucrats have never been confused with Chinese Mandarins, but it is clear that in the past, government employment was quite attractive. The writer Nelson Rodrigues asked then President Kubitschek for a government job and was promised the position of treasurer of the teamsters' pension fund. Fortunately, he flunked an eye examination! On the other hand, it is claimed that these jobs required no work and perhaps they were truly a form of transfer. Nonetheless, the example illustrates that bureaucratic jobs at one point were very attractive, perhaps too much so. Werneck's data, as well as casual observation, show that this is no longer the case, at least in the federal executive branch, where jobs no longer seem capable of attracting quality candidates.

The failure of the repeated attempts at macroeconomic stabilization lies, however, not in implementation but in wretched design. As such, the responsibility lies not with the bureaucracy but with the political class, and with the economists and other pundits who have been so forthcoming in designing "stabilization plans" to satisfy the politicians' fantasies. A team of graduates of the French National Administration School could not help the Cruzado Plan's reliance on the absurd idea that in the Brazilian case, indexation, not monetized deficits, was the cause of inflation. The Collor Plan was doomed from the start by its many inconsistencies, including an elementary confusion between stocks and flows of money. The so-called orthodox stabilization plans that rely on high real interest rates to control inflation, while doing very little to produce a budget surplus, will succeed only when the laws of arithmetic are repealed. Like medieval lords in search of an alchemist to transform lead into gold, the Brazilian political class searches for advisors willing to design a plan for macroeconomic stabilization that does not require unpleasant fiscal adjustments, and the supply of "alchemists" seems inexhaustible.

The New Fiscal Federalism

Like many other observers, Werneck stresses that the 1988 Constitution made it more difficult to pursue the needed fiscal adjustment by transferring sources of income from the federal government to the states. Though this decentralization should have positive long-run effects, it requires that the states take over functions that were traditionally assigned to the central government and are, in the minds of most Brazilians, still the responsibility of Brasilia. While the process of transferring responsibilities is not finished, the states have an unusually easy budgetary situation; however, the fiscal pressure on the federal government is increased. Werneck emphasizes that the constitutional reform scheduled to begin next October should ensure a distribution of fiscal resources that is compatible with the expenditure obligations of each level of government, if it is to create a climate in which economic reforms leading to stability are possible.

Although I agree that the 1988 Constitution needs to be amended to bring fiscal powers and responsibilities across the different levels of government closer into line, I believe that this constitutional change by itself will not accomplish much. The 1990 episode described in the paper makes this point well: despite the new resources, local governments overspent in preparation for elections and were financed by state banks. The bailout of these banks by the Central Bank offset any fiscal austerity efforts by the federal government. This mechanism of transfers from the federal government to the states via the state banks is well known and has been repeatedly used. The federal government has the means to stop these transfers but, as Werneck notes, the state governors once more prevailed. That is, even though the new Constitution mandated that the states receive an unusually high share of total tax revenues, the federal government transferred extra, nonmandated resources via the Central Bank.

This observation makes it tempting to view the federal government and its allies in state governments as a single "Beckerian" family and to conclude that the state banks would have been allowed to finance an even larger state government deficit if the Constitution had mandated that a larger share of the tax revenues accrue to the federal government. In this view, Brasilia transfers resources to its allies in state governments because it thinks that they are more efficient in spending money to keep the coalition in power. Such decentralization protects the few opposition state governments but does not have much of an effect on the aggregate expenditures of the federal government and its allies. The share of expenditures that is allotted to state governments by the Constitution is not currently a binding constraint, and the actual share reflects the political equilibrium of the moment. It goes without saying that controlling the federal government deficit requires that states be forbidden to pursue deficit spending through what essentially amounts to Central Bank financing.

Though I may disagree with Werneck on the extent to which the Constitution is responsible for the present inconsistent fiscal arrangement across jurisdictions, this analysis reinforces his view that economic reforms may depend on the overhaul of electoral legislation to give rise to a majority in Congress committed to a sensible economic policy.

References

Baumol, William J. 1990. Entrepreneurship: Productive, Unproductive, and Destructive. *Journal of Political Economy* 98: 5 (October).

INDEX